Wartime Woodburners

From the author's collection.

Wartime Woodburners

Gas Producer Vehicles in World War II An Overview

John Fuller Ryan

Schiffer Military History
Atglen, PA

Acknowledgments

Many thanks to Paul L. Johnson, who showed the way. Other comrades and colleagues who helped with this effort were Dale Windhorst, Larry Mayo, Malcom Gatford and Joe Tutkowski Jr. Daniel Hagen proved a font of knowledge on the topic, and was very generous with help and advice. The author is very grateful to the able Frederick Schwink for his excellent translation. Finally the author wishes to express his overwhelming gratitude to his beloved wife Susan, without whose patience and support none of this would have been possible.

Book Design by Ian Robertson.

Library of Congress Control Number: 200842153

Printed in China.
ISBN: 978-0-7643-3240-1

We are interested in hearing from authors with book ideas on related topics.

Published by Schiffer Publishing Ltd.
4880 Lower Valley Road
Atglen, PA 19310
Phone: (610) 593-1777
FAX: (610) 593-2002
E-mail: Info@schifferbooks.com.
Visit our web site at: www.schifferbooks.com
Please write for a free catalog.
This book may be purchased from the publisher.
Please include $5.00 postage.
Try your bookstore first.

In Europe, Schiffer books are distributed by:
Bushwood Books
6 Marksbury Avenue
Kew Gardens
Surrey TW9 4JF, England
Phone: 44 (0) 20 8392-8585
FAX: 44 (0) 20 8392-9876
E-mail: Info@bushwoodbooks.co.uk.
Visit our website at: www.bushwoodbooks.co.uk

Contents

An Introduction to Woodburners

In this age of high fuel prices and concern with continuing availability of oil, scientists are working on a number of approaches to alternate fuel sources. These concerns may provoke interest in how some people in gas-starved Europe dealt with such problems beginning in the late 1930s and throughout the war years, 1939-1945.

One of the most successful innovations—keeping many cars on the road which otherwise would have been parked "for the duration"—were the so-called "gas producer" vehicles. Called "gazogene" in French or "Holzvergaser" in German, these vehicles utilized the byproducts of solid fuel combustion, employing such solids as coal, charcoal, turf, and wood to produce fuel gas for a standard internal combustion engine. An example by Mercedes is shown here.

Many people, seeing photographs of these vehicles and learning that they used solid fuel, assume that they operated like a steam engine, that is, by using heat from solid fuel to produce steam, which powered the vehicle. This is not the case.

To understand how the units worked, one must recall some basic principles about combustion. When a substance, let us say wood, burns, the solid substance itself does not produce the heat and light of combustion. What is actually "burning," or rapidly oxidizing, are the gases given off from the heated solid. To observe this light a wooden match, hold it sideways, and carefully observe the area between the matchstick itself and the beginning of the flame. There is a clear, transparent space visible between the shriveling matchstick and the base of the hot, bright flame. This is the area where the combustible gases are being emitted from the heated wood. They do not ignite immediately upon leaving the wood, because at that point the mixture is too "rich" in pure wood gas to burn. At a slightly higher point, as the warm gases rise, enough oxygen from the air mixes with the gases to allow combustion.

Another example is the phenomenon known in the fire service as "backdraft." Let us say a fire starts in an empty home, in a couch, for instance. The fire burns for a while, as the gases and vapors from the heated couch material mix with oxygen in the room and ignite. As the fire continues, oxygen in the room is consumed. If the room is fairly tightly sealed, with the windows and doors tightly closed, the fire will "bank down," i.e. cease emitting heat and light. The couch is still heated, and still giving off potentially flammable gases and vapors, but there is not enough oxygen to allow the vapors to ignite, and they cannot dissipate as the room is sealed. The flammable vapors begin to build up in the room, and the mixture becomes richer in gas and even poorer in oxygen. Heavy smoke forms, and the fire darkens and begins to smolder rather than burn freely, though

Mercedes truck conversion gas producer. Note the black cylinder to the rear of the driver's compartment, the "extra" radiator to the front, and below the extra radiator a long horizontal cylinder. These are all components of the gas producer system. (Reprinted with permission of the Mercedes-Benz Museum)

considerable heat is still present. Some fires actually "burn themselves out" if oxygen is not ultimately admitted. However, in this hypothetical case, let us say the homeowner arrives and unwittingly opens the door to the room. Instantly oxygen rushes in, mixes with the now-concentrated hot flammable gases and vapors, and the entire room explodes into lethal flame. Firefighters avoid this effect by ventilating the room from above, releasing the pent-up gases just before the attack team advances to cool the fire with water.

This "back draft" principle is employed by the solid-fuel gas producer. Solid fuel, like wood, is introduced into the container, the hatch is sealed, and the fuel ignited from below. Admission of oxygen (air) is then controlled through adjustable valves or carefully designed vents. Now, the unit must sit for a time while heat and flammable gases build up inside the sealed container. What is going on inside the container is the same as what happened in our sealed fire room earlier, as the gases concentrate and the fire, rather than blazing up, smolders. Enough air is admitted to keep the process going (i.e. prevent the fire from going out completely), but not enough to allow the gas and vapors to burn freely ("backdraft"), so a richer and richer gas mixture is formed within the sealed container. When enough gas has formed, the heated flammable gases are valved through a series of filters, then through a cooling unit, and finally the gases are piped through a modified or specially adjusted carburetor for admission to the cylinders, where they are explosively ignited by the spark plugs, just as gasoline vapor is in a conventional gasoline engine. In a slightly different adaptation some of the gas is used to run the vehicle, and some is stored in an expandable bladder or low-pressure cylinder for later use, or for demands of acceleration or load greater than the present production of the generator.

One of the commonest and most practical of these systems was designed by the inventor and chemist George Imbert (1884-1950). Imbert's system, called the "Imbert gasifier," could operate either with wood or charcoal, used the downstroke of the engine's pistons to draw air into the heating chamber, and used a small helical fan to propel the gas into the carburetor on start-up. The system was less bulky than some others, and efficient given the limitations of the technology. A schematic of the Imbert system is shown here.

While there were a number of other systems, they all seem to have operated on more or less the same principle, though fuel choice varied a great deal.

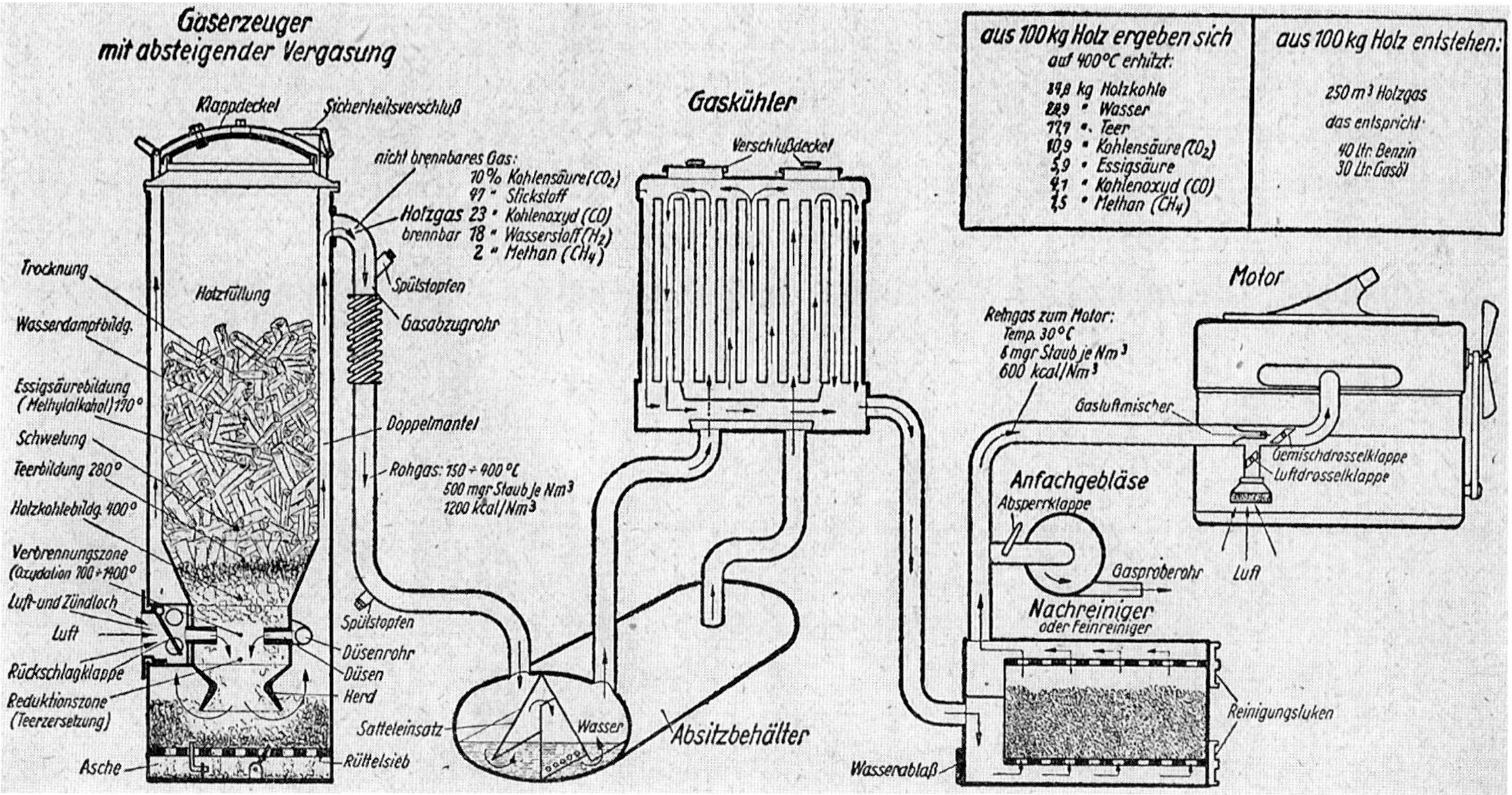

The Imbert unit consists of (from left to right) the boiler or firebox with air injectors near the base. In the middle is the radiator unit used to cool the gases from the firebox, below that a prefilter unit that baffles the gas through water. To the left of that is the large filter which contains oiled wood chips, oiled cork, or some other finely-divided material to remove ash, soot, etc. Above the large filter is the fan used to accelerate gas for startup and an air intake to mix the produced gases with air.

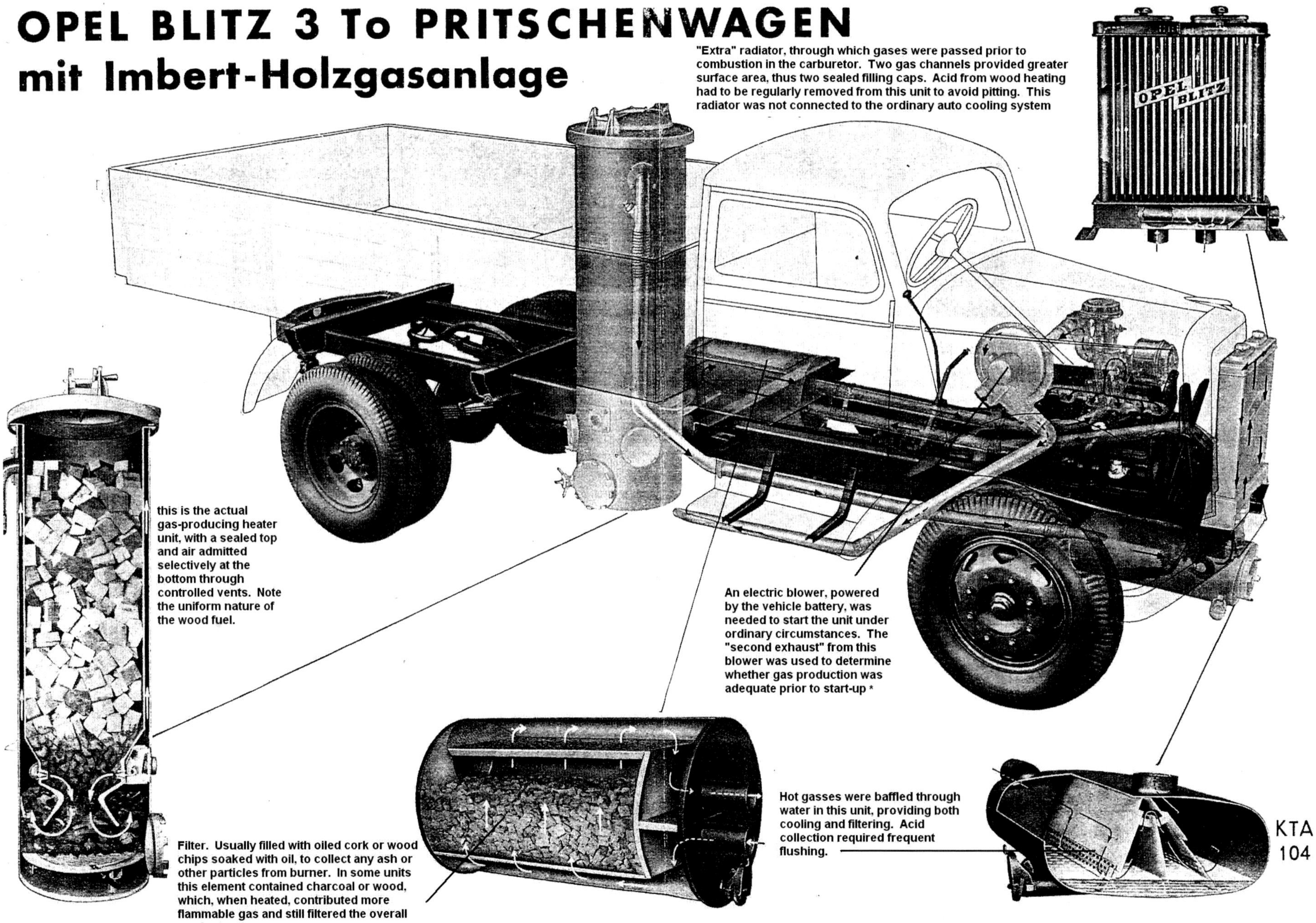

* In very cold weather, or when the battery was low, the vehicle was started first with gasoline, and the gas generator introduced after the vehicle was running.

A schematic of the Imbert Gas Generator demonstrates the chemical reactions created by heating wood in a sealed container. The primary gases created for burning in the engine are Carbon Monoxide and some Methane. The area of very high temperature (1400 °C) is coated with ceramic material to withstand the heat and acids created during combustion. If the fuel were green or resinous wood, like pine, the byproducts produced would include tannic acid and pine tar, both difficult to deal with and liable to damage the unit through clogging, pitting, or deterioration of seals. Therefore, the preferred fuels were dry hardwoods in more-or-less uniform shapes.

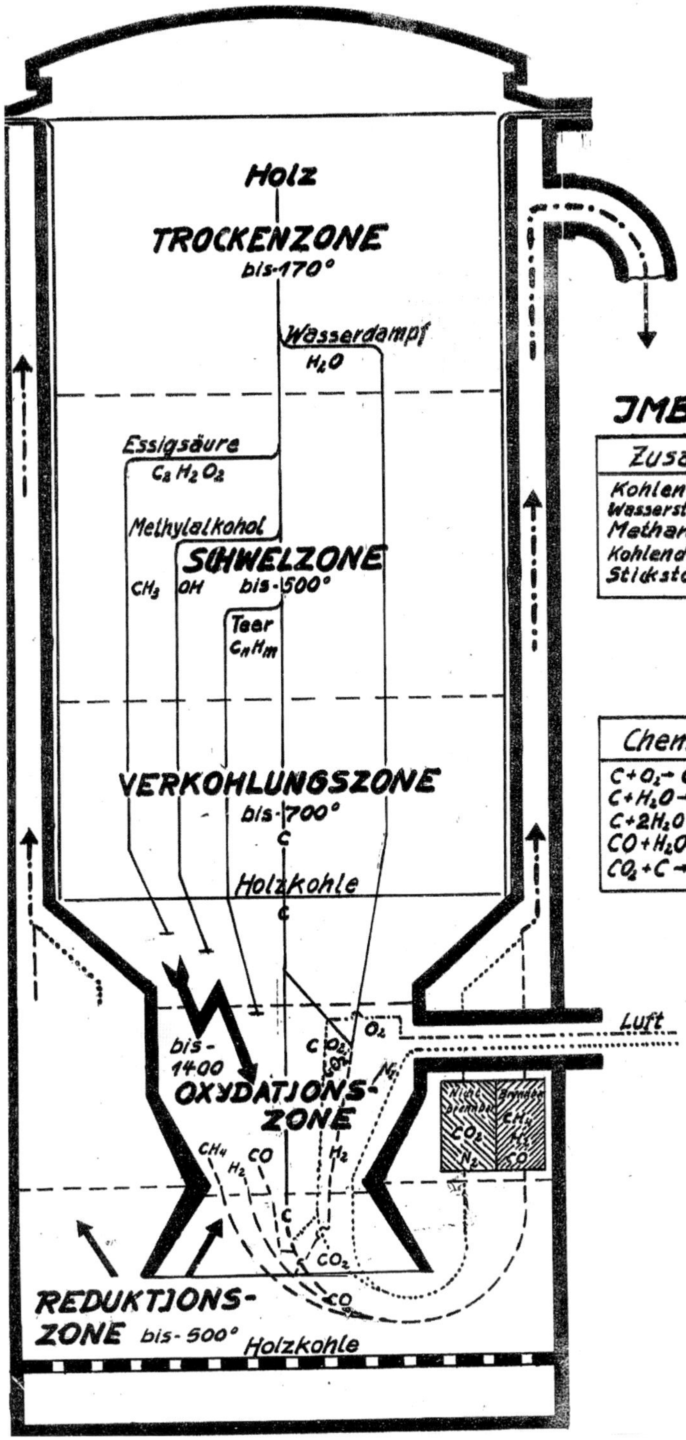

IMBERT-HOLZGAS

Zusammensetzung:		
Kohlenoxyd	CO	23 %
Wasserstoff	H_2	18 %
Methan	CH_4	2 %
Kohlendioxyd	CO_2	10 %
Stickstoff	N_2	47 %

Chemische Formeln:	
$C + O_2 \rightarrow CO_2$	Oxydation (+Wärme)
$C + H_2O \rightarrow CO + H_2$ ...	Wasserstoff-bildung (-Wärme)
$C + 2H_2O \rightarrow CO_2 + 2H_2$	
$CO + H_2O \rightleftharpoons CO_2 + H_2$	
$CO_2 + C \rightarrow 2CO$ ..	Reduktion (-Wärme)

Abb.6

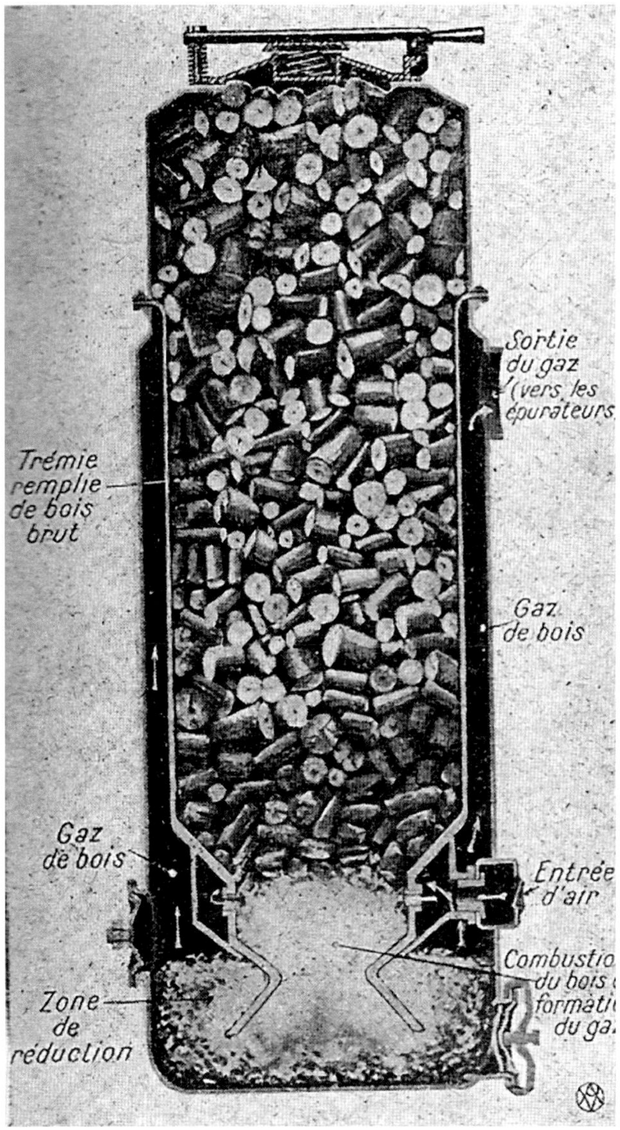

Cutaway of an Imbert gas producer from a French wartime manual demonstrates the size and shape of preferred fuel.

As the reader can imagine, a driver did not just leap up out of bed, grab his keys, and drive off with his gas producer car. A driver had to lug the heavy fuel, heft extra fuel sacks onto the roof of the car, stoke the boiler, light the boiler, wait while gas built up, test for proper gas mixture, shake the grates to clear ash, negotiate the tricky start-up procedure, and only finally drive slowly off.

The fuel was not free. Wood burned in a gas producer could not just be logs or branches. To avoid hot or cold spots and promote proper feeding of fuel in the firebox, the wood had to be "pelletized" (of uniform size and shape), and for best effect the wood had to be dry, either aged or kiln-dried. The wood fuel was often about the size of a child's small alphabet block, and had to have only 20% moisture by volume. Therefore specially-prepared fuel had to be procured at a "Tankholzstelle" (German) or a "Carboto" (French) dealer. A French "filling station" listing for these vehicles is seen here.

Fuel choice determined the gases produced.*

Fuel	CO%	H2%	CO2%	Cal/Kg
Wood (green)	20	20	15	1,820
Wood (dry)	24	20	11	2,230
Charcoal	34	7	1	1,000

(Chart derived from *Les Vehicules equipes avec Gazogene*, Henri Petit, Dunod Publishers, 92 Rue Bonaparte, Paris, 1941, p 40-41)

*All highly variable depending upon preparation of fuel and design of burner. Dryness of wood is uncontrollable variable. Figures are general. Note universally high CO content.

"Carboto" charcoal supplier list of available fuel stations dated March 1938. In France, infrastructure for wood-fueled vehicles seems to have been significant even before the outbreak of war.

Gas producers were not very fast* (speed depending on weight and other factors), and they consumed about 1.5 lb of wood per mile. Therefore, if one had a 15lb sack of "Tankholz" (tank-wood) then one's car had a range of about 10 miles; thus, the practice of carrying extra fuel sacks in a roof rack. Put another way, about 2.5 kilos of specially prepared wood fuel was the equivalent of a liter of gasoline. Given that a liter of fuel weighs about two pounds, and 2.5 kilo is equal to about the same weight, it would seem equivalent. However, 2.5 kilo of wood blocks or charcoal is much bulkier than 1 liter of gasoline. If charcoal was used the process was messier, and of course coal was heavy and messier still. Disposal of residual ash was always a problem, and a potential fire hazard as well as a nuisance.

The woodburners also required special skills of the driver, and incorporated an extra set of controls to regulate air flow, firebox temperature, and so forth. Therefore, special licenses and permits were required to operate these units (see next for a German example), and permits were also required to allow conversion of gasoline vehicles. Fees for these permits and the costs of conversion were significant.

The units were also excruciatingly maintenance intensive. On a regular basis, water had to be drained from condensation traps, filter materials removed and either cleaned or replaced, gaskets treated with sealant, ashes removed and disposed of, carburetor adjusted, and on and on. Accumulation of acid products from the breakdown of wood was always a problem. See the appendix for a translation of a typical maintenance schedule.

* In Sweden, where the country was extremely dependent on gas producer vehicles (25% of the national fleet used these systems), gasoline was reserved for police cars, ambulances, and fire engines, because gas-producer vehicles were considered too slow. However, this statement may not refer to road speed, but to the time it required for these vehicles to build up sufficient gas once ignited.

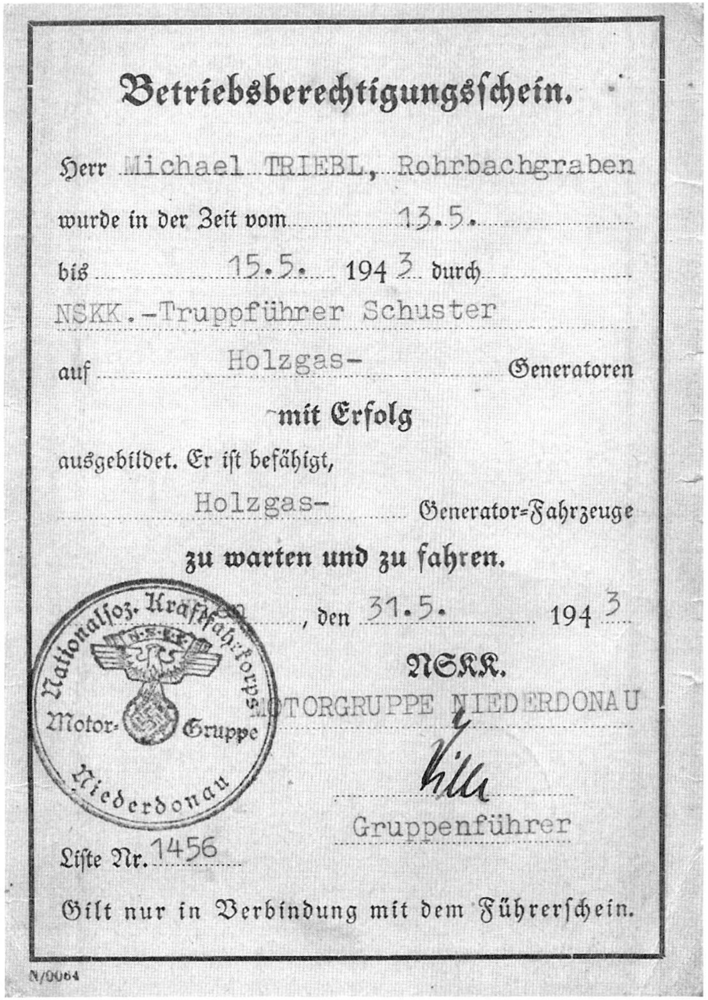

Betriebsberechtigungsschein.

Herr Michael TRIEBL, Rohrbachgraben
wurde in der Zeit vom 13.5.
bis 15.5. 1943 durch
NSKK.-Truppführer Schuster
auf Holzgas- Generatoren
mit Erfolg
ausgebildet. Er ist befähigt,
Holzgas- Generator-Fahrzeuge
zu warten und zu fahren.

Nationalsoz. Kraftfahr-Korps Motor-Gruppe Niederdonau

..., den 31.5. 1943

NSKK.
MOTORGRUPPE NIEDERDONAU

Gruppenführer

Liste Nr. 1456

Gilt nur in Verbindung mit dem Führerschein.

N/0064

German supplementary drivers license stamped "Holz" for "holzvergaser." This supplement was valid only with one's regular driving license. This license was issued in 1943 and bears the stamp of the NSKK, the German Auto organization. The NSKK had the task of driver training. (From the author's collection.)

The systems were frequently bulky, often unattractive, cranky, and dangerous, fire danger being the most obvious. Aside from fire, the units produced as much as 34% carbon monoxide which, though hopefully consumed in the motor, precluded their operation indoors. Even a slight leak of carbon monoxide at those concentrations is rapidly lethal. If a driver stopped for a while, it was sometimes best to leave the unit running (start-up was always tricky), which increased fuel consumption, and exposed the driver to CO if there was even a small leak. Even if the driver switched the engine off (and indeed there were some units which were started with gasoline and then switched to producer gas after startup) the firebox had to be left burning, as build up of heat and sufficient gases from a cold unit could take 10 minutes or more. To top all of this danger and inconvenience off, since the systems were front or rear mounted, the implications of a crash while sitting close to a 1400°C heat source were sobering indeed.

"The systems were bulky, often unattractive..." This view of a "holzvergaser" unit on a German pre-war Opel truck displays the central elements of such units. Mounted forward is the "extra" radiator which cooled the gas from the "boiler" or firebox located behind it. Below the firebox is a long horizontal cylinder that acts as a filter to remove soot, ash, and other contaminants before the gas reaches the carburetor. The filter has a hatch so that filter can be cleaned and the filtering material changed. The hatch just below the "extra" radiator is for the removal of ashes and other unburned residual products. Since the entire system had to be nearly airtight, attention was constantly required to gaskets and seals. Heating of wood produced various acids, which attacked rubber sealing materials. (Reprinted with permission of the photographer.)

Why, then, would people invest in, and deal with the disadvantages of such a system? In short, by 1942 there was no other choice if one wished to remain mobile.

At the beginning of World War II in 1939, Germany had acquired a considerable reserve of fuel, and had taken steps to attempt self-sufficiency in that area. Though lacking domestic sources of oil, Germany had developed a process of creating gasoline fuel from chemical conversion of coal, and Germany had lots of coal.* Also, Germany had managed to store large quantities of fuel, concealing the fact through various subterfuges in order to deceive the world of her aggressive intentions. The "Anschluss" (Occupation of Austria) made more crude oil available to the Reich. Alliances with Hungary, Rumania, and the USSR ensured a steady supply of oil, and indeed the USSR was shipping oil to Germany on the very eve of Germany's invasion. In 1940, after the successful invasion of France, Germany acquired even greater oil supply, taking over significant sources in Alsace. There was relatively little domestic civilian consumption of fuel in Germany, there being only 1 passenger vehicle for 52 people in Germany, as opposed to a ratio of 1:18 in the UK and 1:5 in the U.S. Therefore, German fuel resources were available almost exclusively to the military.

In addition, the German army was not as heavily mechanized as conventional wisdom would have it. In fact, the German army of WWII was 80% foot-marching or horse drawn, another factor to consider when contemplating Germany's fuel position. For example, the invading German army entered the USSR with about 750,000 horses.

Thus, in 1940 Germany was in an adequate position regarding fuel, and in the words of one expert:

"Without question 6.6 million tons of crude and refined petroleum would easily have satisfied any and all domestic projects upon which the Third Reich might embark, ***were she only able to curb her obsession for additional conquest*** (emphasis added)."

*Though coal gasification is considerably more expensive (perhaps as much as four times as expensive) than other means of supply, Germany, having been blockaded and fuel-starved during WWI, felt the investment was worth it.

German supply column of Saurer 4.5 ton trucks pushes forward on a dusty, rutted Russian road. Road conditions in Russia were extremely unkind to carefully-machined German trucks, as their suspensions, transmissions, and cooling systems broke down under these primitive conditions, but worse was yet to come. (From the author's collection.)

Of course, Germany was unable to "curb her obsession for additional conquest," and on June 22, 1941, Germany invaded the Soviet Union. When the German army entered the USSR 800,000 vehicles were consuming fuel. The Germans, in June 1941, used 268,000 metric tons of gasoline and 86,000 metric tons of diesel fuel. The *Luftwaffe* projected a drain of 250,000 metric tons of expensive aviation fuel per month. Compare this with the consumption of 100,000 metric tons per month during the Polish and French campaigns and the Battle of Britain, and you have an idea of the awesome scale of the German invasion.

The vast distances and poor roads of Russia gobbled fuel. Trucks had to be used to supply armored spearheads because Russian railway gauges did not match those of Germany, and German locomotives could not operate using Russian coal. The Soviets had either evacuated domestic railroad rolling stock or destroyed it. Breakdowns became frequent, as trucks designed for paved European highways foundered in the dust, sand, and mud of the USSR. German production vehicles were finely made and maintenance intensive, and much waste occurred in towing breakdowns to repair areas. Autumn rains began, and the primitive Russian roads disappeared as the "***Schlammperiod***" (German for "Mud Season") commenced.

Wehrmacht staff cars founder in soupy Russian mud. A heavy semi- tracked vehicle is coming to the rescue. (Courtesy Paul L. Johnson)

Trucks, cars, and even tanks sank to their axles in bottomless mud, again increasing fuel consumption as vehicles revved, bogged, and slithered on these slimy surfaces. Expensive aircraft fuel had to be used as transport planes ferried supplies to stranded panzer columns. Even fodder for horses had to be moved by aircraft. (For an outstanding study of the German army's dependence on the horse, see the excellent Schiffer publication *Horses of the German Army in World War II*, by Paul L. Johnson.)

Then came winter.

German troops struggle to extricate vehicles trapped in snow. (From the author's collection.)

The story of the misery of the *Wehrmacht* in the winter of 1941-42 has often been told, and I will not elaborate except to recount some of the fuel problems caused by the weather. Oils solidified in the punishing cold, and vehicles fractured crankshafts and bearings if cranked with frozen oil. Batteries lost power. Radiators, even those equipped with conventional European antifreeze, froze solid.

Overnight, every vehicle had to be frequently started and idled when not in use. Crankcases had to be warmed with gasoline-powered torches. Troops huddled around gasoline fires or used vehicle heaters to try to keep warm. Trucks laboring on icy roads or idling in huge traffic jams burned extra fuel, as did motorized snowplows and towing units extricating vehicles trapped in snowdrifts. Fuel-guzzling tracked and semi-tracked vehicles were overused as the only reliable mobility under these conditions. In short, fuel consumption skyrocketed.

Many improvisations were employed to try to keep engines and batteries warm. In this photo, a captured Soviet ZIS truck in German service is protected with a hood blanket of woven straw. (From the author's collection.)

Very quickly Germany's treasured fuel reserves were gone; she was consuming fuel faster than even coal gasification and her allies could produce it, and Germany turned to occupied Europe for supply. Fuel supplies in Holland, France, Norway, Denmark, Poland, and Greece, already minimal due to earlier domestic military demand, began to dry up entirely as Germany simply looted gasoline stocks. A British wartime report states that after meeting the needs of Germany's fighting forces there remained in Europe in 1943 "some 7 million tons of oil to supply a need formerly met by 26 million tons." Therefore, according to the same study:

"In these circumstances, Germany has been equally the arbiter of the destiny of Europe's oil supplies, as she has been of all other resources. After taking the 12 to 13 millions of tons of oil required annually for her fighting forces and for her civilian population, the remainder has been allocated in such quantities as are no more than sufficient to ensure maximum productivity of industry in occupied countries as are serving German ends, ***and to provide the minimum required to prevent a complete breakdown in essential services*** (emphasis added)."

Neutral Sweden was cut off from imported fuel due to closing of the sea lanes. England, under threat of isolation from submarines and experiencing its own military demands, also severely curtailed civilian use of motor fuel.

The humble, wheezing gas producer vehicle, employed only minimally before the war, was now "an idea whose time had come."

At first, the gas producer units were mostly built by individual mechanics or small shops. Later, as the units proved relatively efficient and popular, commercial firms and auto manufacturers began to produce standardized commercial versions. In France, these "gazogene" began to assume a very sleek, even elegant, appearance.

This vehicle appears to be an Opel Wanderer, fitted with what looks like a locally-manufactured (i.e. not commercially standardized) gas producer system. Note again the primary features: Large cylindrical sealed boiler or firebox, roof rack with extra sacks of fuel, filter to the right of firebox, and convoluted piping carrying gas forward to the engine. (Photo courtesy Paul Hagen)

This purpose-built "Panhard" gazogene is not yet streamlined, but the design is cleaner, and the unit includes a covered roof-rack for fuel. (From the author's collection.)

This elegant sedan hides the bulky apparatus in the elongated trunk, and demonstrates the rapid evolution of design of gas-producer vehicles. (From the author's collection.)

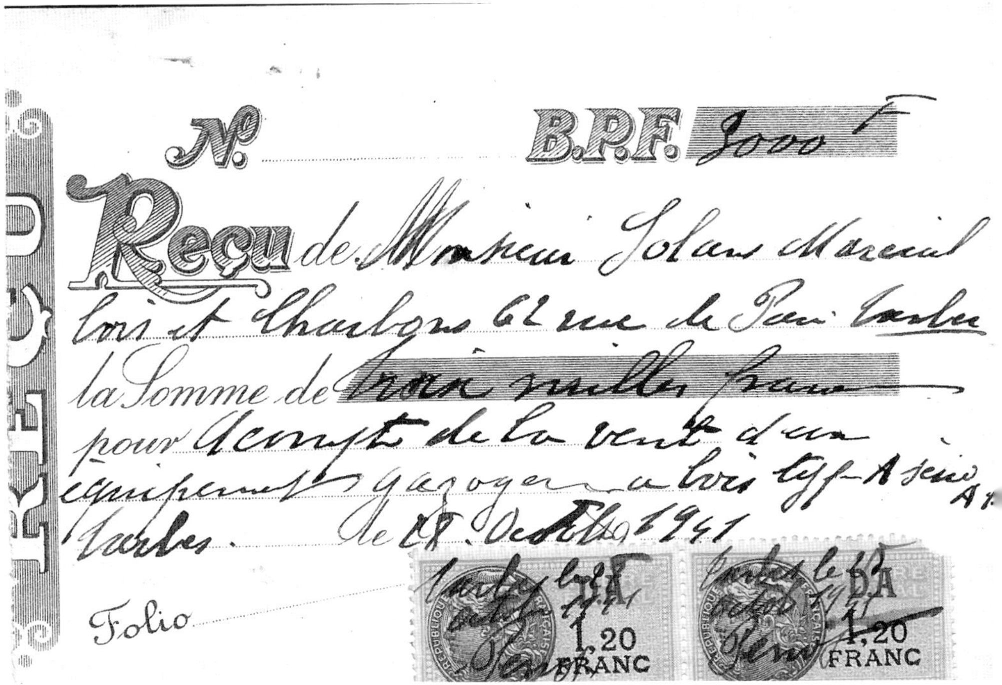

N°

B.P.F. 3000 F

Reçu de Monsieur Solans Marcial
bois et charbons 62 rue de Paris Tarbes
la Somme de trois mille francs
pour acompte de la vente d'un
équipement gazogène à bois type A série A
Tarbes le 28 Octobre 1941

Folio

1,20 FRANC 1,20 FRANC

Receipt for purchase of a "gazogene" in 1941. At 2000 Francs, this is fairly expensive. (From the author's collection.)

A Few Facts and Figures About Fuel

In October 1942, Albert Speer spoke about the need to conserve fuel by converting gasoline vehicles to solid-fuel vehicles:

"I refer on that the supply status for fluid fuels. All operators of utility vehicles will find it in their own interest for transportation or business, to transpose their vehicles to generator gas. He who does not convert his vehicle cannot be assured whether Gasoline or diesel fuel will be hereafter available."

In 1942 conversion saved 5 million tons of liquid fuel. By 1943 8 million tons of fuel had been conserved.

In France, gasoline was available to physicians, midwives, police, fire agencies, and other government entities. Due to vehicle conversion and other demands, production of charcoal for vehicle fuel increased from 50,000 tons/year prewar to 500,000 tons/year by 1943. There were 50,000 *gazogenes* in France in 1941, 120,000 by 1944. There were also 2 million bicycles in Paris by 1944, per Pechanski and Durand's *Collaboration and Resistance*.

French woodburner refilling station sign.

German fuel dealer advertisement.

Albert Speer, shown here to Hitler's left, was Hitler's architect, but also put in charge of war production. Speer's efforts to rationalize German industry undoubtedly allowed Germany to continue the war longer than she could otherwise have done.

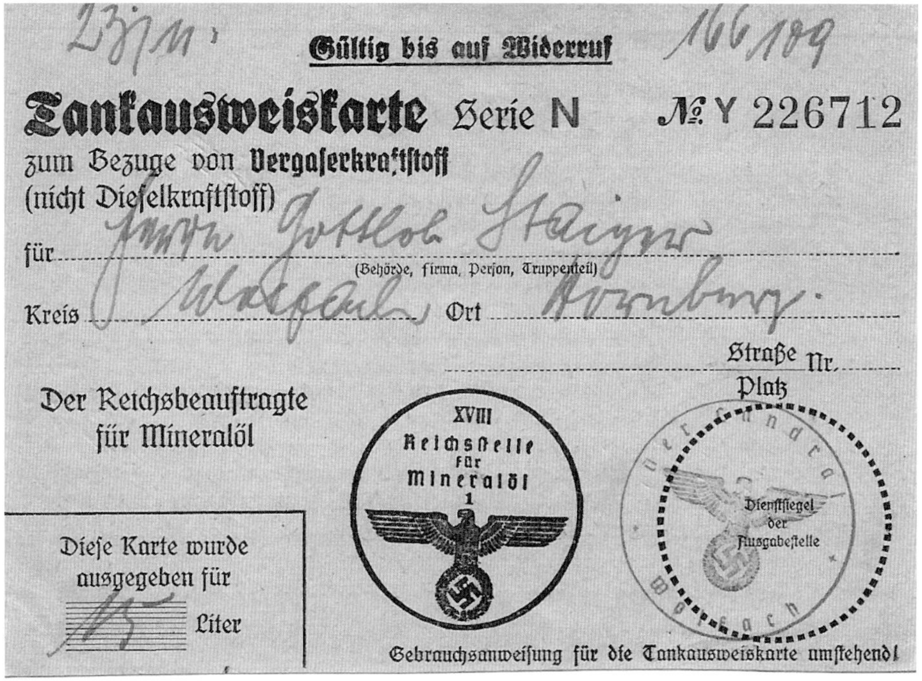

Gültig bis auf Widerruf

Tankausweiskarte Serie N №Y 226712

zum Bezuge von **Vergaserkraftstoff**
(nicht Dieselkraftstoff)

für ....
(Behörde, Firma, Person, Truppenteil)

Kreis .... Ort ....

Straße Nr.
Platz

Der Reichsbeauftragte
für Mineralöl

XVIII Reichsstelle für Mineralöl 1

Dienstsiegel der Ausgabestelle

Diese Karte wurde ausgegeben für .... Liter

Gebrauchsanweisung für die Tankausweiskarte umstehend!

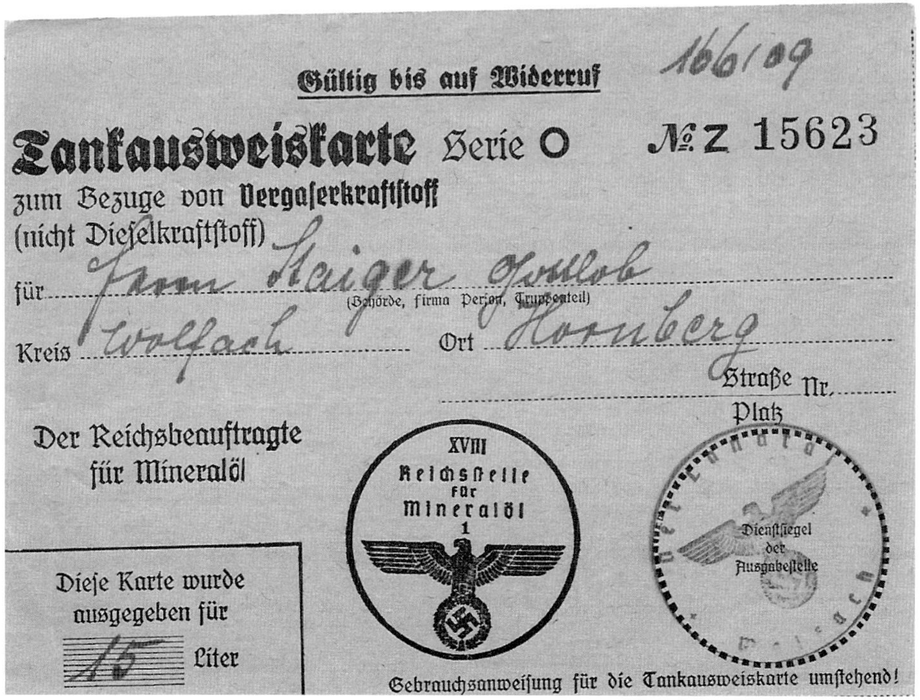

Gültig bis auf Widerruf

Tankausweiskarte Serie O №Z 15623

zum Bezuge von **Vergaserkraftstoff**
(nicht Dieselkraftstoff)

für ....
(Behörde, Firma, Person, Truppenteil)

Kreis .... Ort ....

Straße Nr.
Platz

Der Reichsbeauftragte
für Mineralöl

XVIII Reichsstelle für Mineralöl 1

Dienstsiegel der Ausgabestelle

Diese Karte wurde ausgegeben für .... Liter

Gebrauchsanweisung für die Tankausweiskarte umstehend!

German gasoline ration tickets.

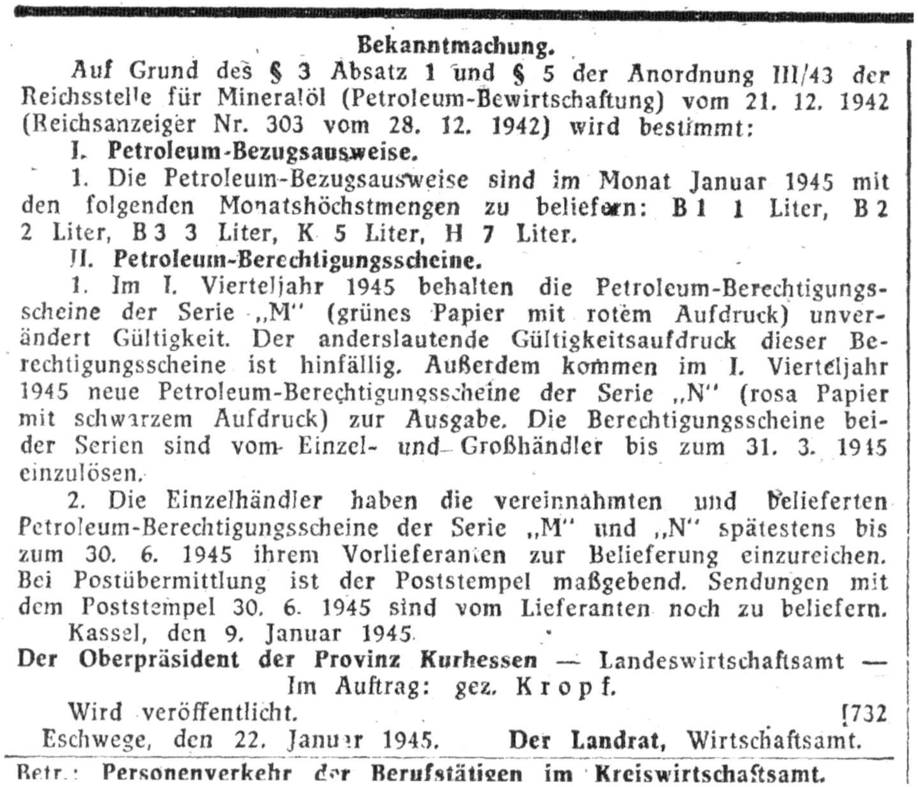

Bekanntmachung.

Auf Grund des § 3 Absatz 1 und § 5 der Anordnung III/43 der Reichsstelle für Mineralöl (Petroleum-Bewirtschaftung) vom 21. 12. 1942 (Reichsanzeiger Nr. 303 vom 28. 12. 1942) wird bestimmt:

I. Petroleum-Bezugsausweise.

1. Die Petroleum-Bezugsausweise sind im Monat Januar 1945 mit den folgenden Monatshöchstmengen zu beliefern: **B 1** 1 Liter, **B 2** 2 Liter, **B 3** 3 Liter, **K** 5 Liter, **H** 7 Liter.

II. Petroleum-Berechtigungsscheine.

1. Im I. Vierteljahr 1945 behalten die Petroleum-Berechtigungsscheine der Serie „M" (grünes Papier mit rotem Aufdruck) unverändert Gültigkeit. Der anderslautende Gültigkeitsaufdruck dieser Berechtigungsscheine ist hinfällig. Außerdem kommen im I. Vierteljahr 1945 neue Petroleum-Berechtigungsscheine der Serie „N" (rosa Papier mit schwarzem Aufdruck) zur Ausgabe. Die Berechtigungsscheine beider Serien sind vom Einzel- und Großhändler bis zum 31. 3. 1945 einzulösen.

2. Die Einzelhändler haben die vereinnahmten und belieferten Petroleum-Berechtigungsscheine der Serie „M" und „N" spätestens bis zum 30. 6. 1945 ihrem Vorlieferanten zur Belieferung einzureichen. Bei Postübermittlung ist der Poststempel maßgebend. Sendungen mit dem Poststempel 30. 6. 1945 sind vom Lieferanten noch zu beliefern.

Kassel, den 9. Januar 1945.

Der Oberpräsident der Provinz Kurhessen — Landeswirtschaftsamt —
Im Auftrag: gez. K r o p f.

Wird veröffentlicht. [732

Eschwege, den 22. Januar 1945. **Der Landrat,** Wirtschaftsamt.

Betr.: **Personenverkehr der Berufstätigen im Kreiswirtschaftsamt.**

German ration allocations for each quarter were published in newspapers, informing ration ticket holders of the amount of fuel they could expect for their ration documents. This procedure was preferable to issuing new ration books and so forth every four months. The notice above informs consumers in Kurhessen province what their fuel allocation would be for the first quarter of 1945. The notice also informs distributors exactly which ration forms are now valid. Even if one held the correct documents, however, fuel might not be available for purchase, due to rail disruptions and so forth.

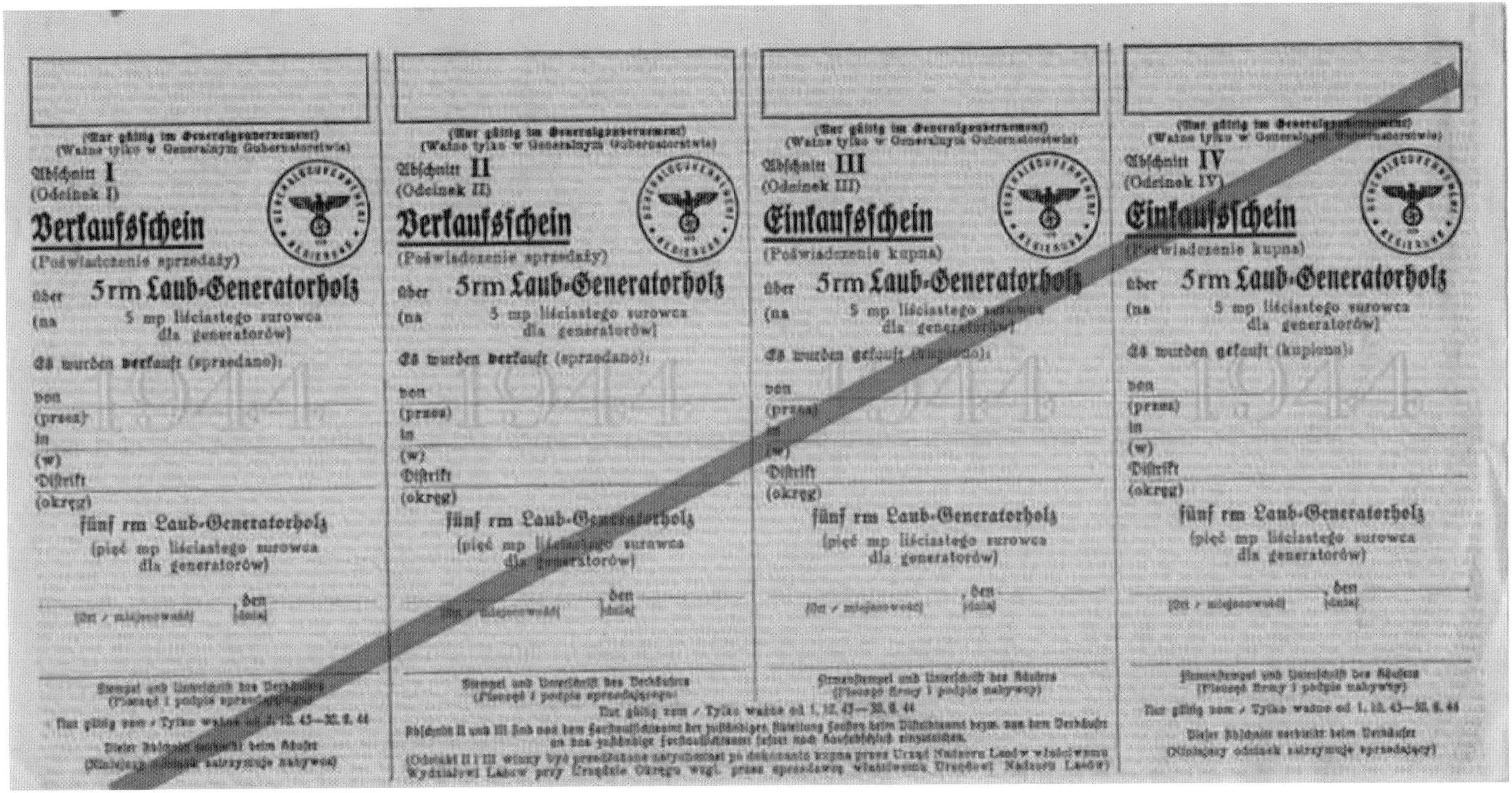

Abschnitt I
(Odcinek I)
Verkaufsschein
(Poświadczenie sprzedaży)
über 5rm Laub-Generatorholz
(na 5 mp liściastego surowca dla generatorów)
Es wurden verkauft (sprzedano):
von
(przez)
in
(w)
Distrikt
(okręg)
fünf rm Laub-Generatorholz
(pięć mp liściastego surowca dla generatorów)

Abschnitt II
(Odcinek II)
Verkaufsschein
(Poświadczenie sprzedaży)
über 5rm Laub-Generatorholz
(na 5 mp liściastego surowca dla generatorów)
Es wurden verkauft (sprzedano):
von
(przez)
in
(w)
Distrikt
(okręg)
fünf rm Laub-Generatorholz
(pięć mp liściastego surowca dla generatorów)

Abschnitt III
(Odcinek III)
Einkaufsschein
(Poświadczenie kupna)
über 5rm Laub-Generatorholz
(na 5 mp liściastego surowca dla generatorów)
Es wurden gekauft
von
in
(w)
Distrikt
(okręg)
fünf rm Laub-Generatorholz
(pięć mp liściastego surowca dla generatorów)

Abschnitt IV
(Odcinek IV)
Einkaufsschein
(Poświadczenie kupna)
über 5rm Laub-Generatorholz
(na 5 mp liściastego surowca dla generatorów)
Es wurden gekauft (kupiono):
von
(przez)
in
(w)
Distrikt
(okręg)
fünf rm Laub-Generatorholz
(pięć mp liściastego surowca dla generatorów)

Of course, like nearly everything else in Occupied Europe, fuel wood ("Tankholz") was also rationed. Shown above are ration stamps from what the Germans called the "General Government" - Poland. Each stamp allows the holder to purchase 5 Reichsmarks worth of "Laub-Tankholz," which is presumably fuel wood made from branches and limbs. The paper is embossed and watermarked to prevent forgery, and the green stripe probably has a similar function. Once again, though, having the proper stamps did not guarantee actual delivery of the product, as any number of factors, not the least of which was preemptive military demand, could alter supply. (Courtesy MAR Historical)

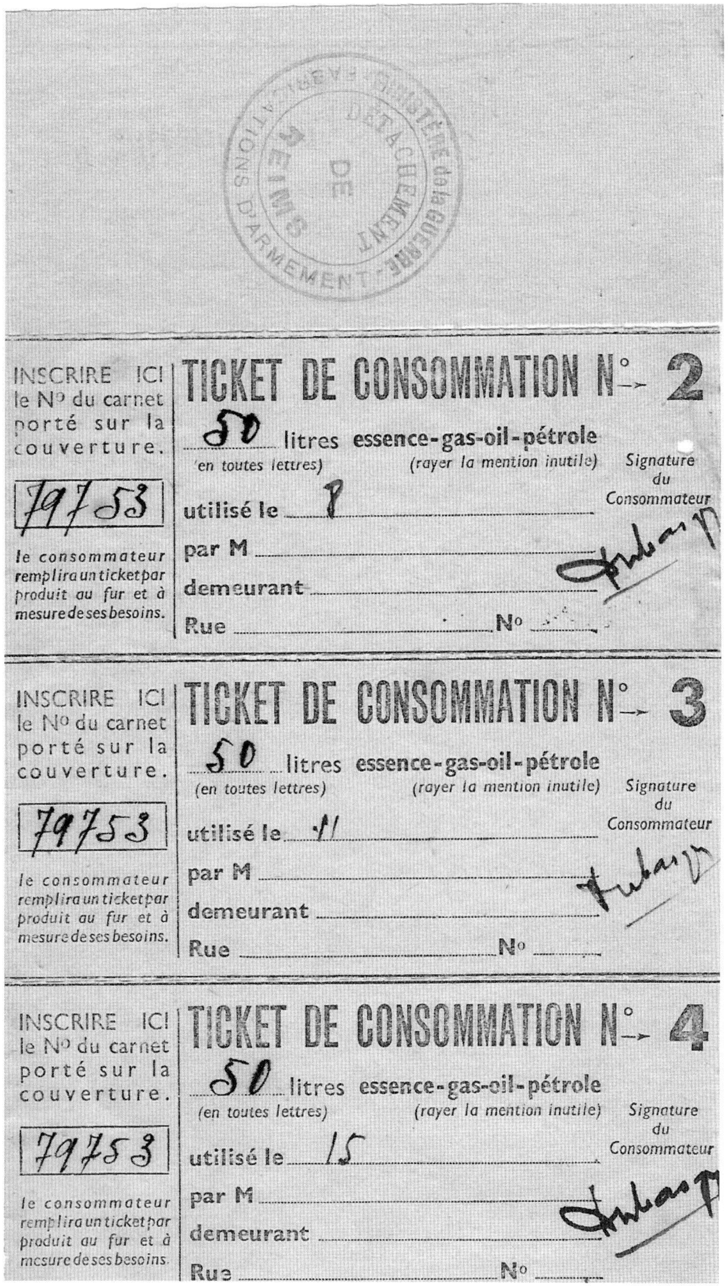

DÉTACHEMENT DE REIMS

INSCRIRE ICI le N° du carnet porté sur la couverture. 79753

le consommateur remplira un ticket par produit au fur et à mesure de ses besoins.

TICKET DE CONSOMMATION N° 2

50 litres essence-gas-oil-pétrole
(en toutes lettres) (rayer la mention inutile)

Signature du Consommateur

utilisé le 8
par M
demeurant
Rue N°

INSCRIRE ICI le N° du carnet porté sur la couverture. 79753

le consommateur remplira un ticket par produit au fur et à mesure de ses besoins.

TICKET DE CONSOMMATION N° 3

50 litres essence-gas-oil-pétrole
(en toutes lettres) (rayer la mention inutile)

Signature du Consommateur

utilisé le 11
par M
demeurant
Rue N°

INSCRIRE ICI le N° du carnet porté sur la couverture. 79753

le consommateur remplira un ticket par produit au fur et à mesure de ses besoins.

TICKET DE CONSOMMATION N° 4

50 litres essence-gas-oil-pétrole
(en toutes lettres) (rayer la mention inutile)

Signature du Consommateur

utilisé le 15
par M
demeurant
Rue N°

Right: Shown here is a permit to operate a Citroen Camionette (very small truck) using "Gaz de Ville" ("city gas," probably Propane, perhaps Methane) in the city of Paris. Such documents are typical of the sort of bureaucracy that Europeans were accustomed to.

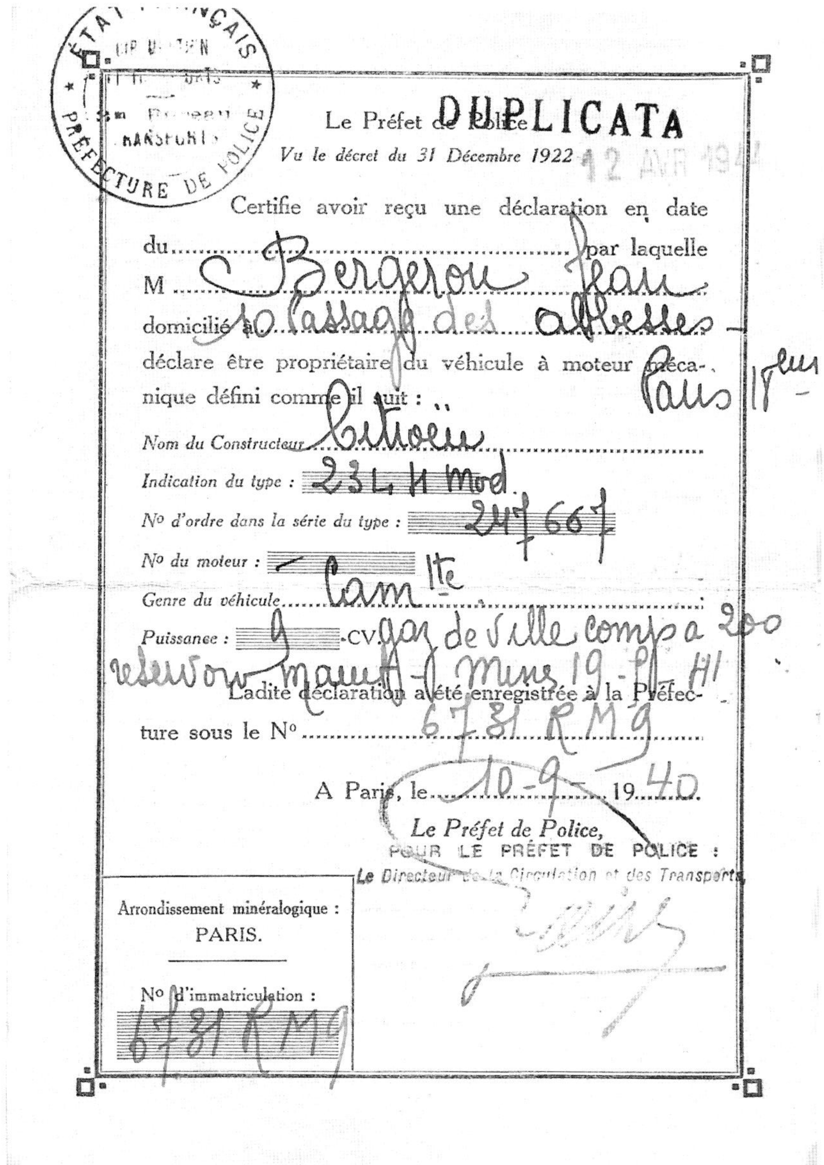

ÉTAT FRANÇAIS — PRÉFECTURE DE POLICE

DUPLICATA

Le Préfet de Police

Vu le décret du 31 Décembre 1922

12 AVR 1941

Certifie avoir reçu une déclaration en date du .... par laquelle M Bergeron Jean domicilié à 10 Passage des Abbesses – Paris 18ème déclare être propriétaire du véhicule à moteur mécanique défini comme il suit :

Nom du Constructeur Citroën

Indication du type : 23 L H Mod

N° d'ordre dans la série du type : 247667

N° du moteur : –

Genre du véhicule Cam lte

Puissance : 9 CV gaz de ville comp à 200

réservoir ... 19-11-41

La dite déclaration a été enregistrée à la Préfecture sous le N° 6731 RM9

A Paris, le 10-9-1940

Le Préfet de Police,
POUR LE PRÉFET DE POLICE :
Le Directeur de la Circulation et des Transports

Arrondissement minéralogique : PARIS.

N° d'immatriculation : 6731 RM9

French Ration Coupons
The top image is the back of a coupon granting a generous 80 Liters. The back of the coupon is stamped by the office of the Minister of War, division of Armament Manufacture, which might explain the size of the ration.

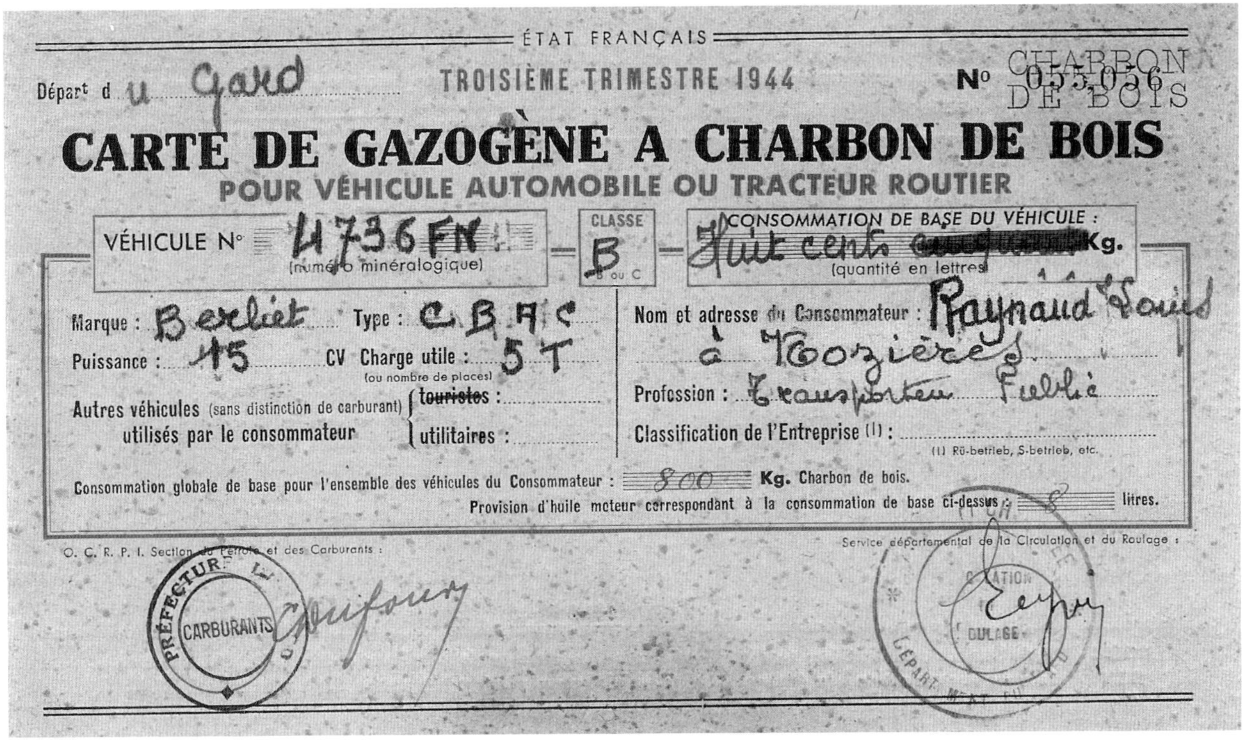

ÉTAT FRANÇAIS

Départ d u Gard TROISIÈME TRIMESTRE 1944 N° 055,056 CHARBON DE BOIS

CARTE DE GAZOGÈNE A CHARBON DE BOIS

POUR VÉHICULE AUTOMOBILE OU TRACTEUR ROUTIER

VÉHICULE N° 4736FN (numéro minéralogique) — CLASSE B (B ou C) — CONSOMMATION DE BASE DU VÉHICULE : Huit cents Kg. (quantité en lettres)

Marque : Berliet Type : CBAC

Puissance : 15 CV Charge utile : 5 T (ou nombre de places)

Autres véhicules (sans distinction de carburant) utilisés par le consommateur { touristes : … utilitaires : …

Nom et adresse du Consommateur : Raynaud Louis à Vozières

Profession : Transporteur Public

Classification de l'Entreprise (1) : …

(1) Rü-betrieb, S-betrieb, etc.

Consommation globale de base pour l'ensemble des véhicules du Consommateur : 800 Kg. Charbon de bois.

Provision d'huile moteur correspondant à la consommation de base ci-dessus : 8 litres.

O. C. R. P. I. Section du Pétrole et des Carburants :

PRÉFECTURE … CARBURANTS

Service départemental de la Circulation et du Roulage :

Document to Track the Use of Fuel
Face sheet of a log kept by a delivery driver, who was allocated 800 kg of charcoal and 8 liters of oil for the third trimester of 1944. (From the author's collection.)

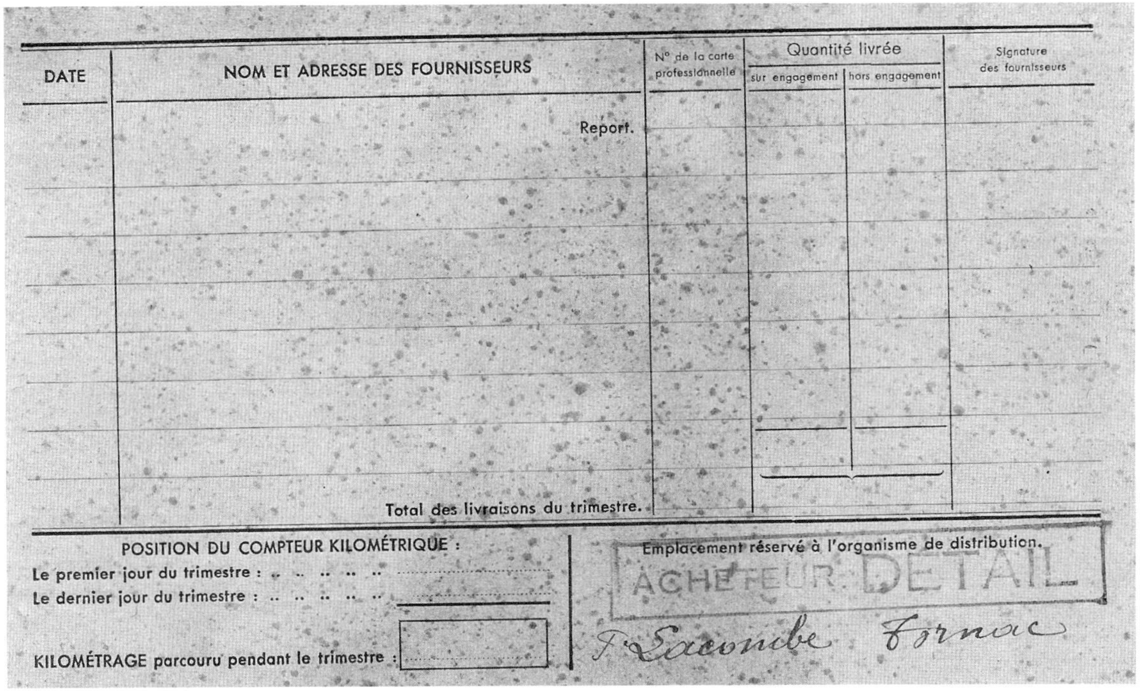

DATE	NOM ET ADRESSE DES FOURNISSEURS	N° de la carte professionnelle	Quantité livrée sur engagement	Quantité livrée hors engagement	Signature des fournisseurs
	Report.				
	Total des livraisons du trimestre.				

POSITION DU COMPTEUR KILOMÉTRIQUE :
Le premier jour du trimestre : …
Le dernier jour du trimestre : …

KILOMÉTRAGE parcouru pendant le trimestre :

Emplacement réservé à l'organisme de distribution.
ACHETEUR DETAIL

Inside page of fuel-use log, which required the driver to list deliveries and the kilometers driven for each. This was to assure that the fuel was being used for business, not for pleasure. Even after the liberation of France fuel was scarce. (From the author's collection.)

A Renault truck and a Ford Eiffel (?) automobile outside a French garage. The truck has a nice factory installation with a handy ladder for fuelling, and the auto features the usual roof rack for fuel and spare tire. The spare tire had to be carried on the roof since the woodburner assembly occupied the trunk space.

No catalog of alternative fuel vehicles would be complete without reference to the classic Citroen "Traction Avant," shown in hundreds of films and vintage photos with gas cylinders on the roof or in tow. Though called "Gazogene" by the French, these vehicles did not *create* gas, but carried compressed flammable gas as fuel. Methane, Acetylene, stove gas (Propane), or any other gas that would burn served as fuel. The utility of these vehicles was limited by the availability of flammable gas, access to compressors, and supplies of scarce steel for cylinders. Thousands have been reproduced in plastic scale models, often with the emblem of the Free French whitewashed on the door. As fuel dried up everywhere, Europeans learned that the sound of a gasoline engine, rather than the throaty stutter of a "gazogene," meant an official visit. Often such a visit was not good news. Enforcement agencies like the *Gestapo* preferred the Citroen, and agencies of that sort had access to gasoline. (From the author's collection.)

Other Citroens were in fact converted to true gas generators. This is a 1938 Traction Avant with an innovative coal burning unit installed by FAP Elgazo Tarbes. On the right fender is the burner unit. The filter is beneath the car, and on the left fender are the cleanouts, cooler, and other components. Because of the small capacity of the gas generator, this vehicle was limited to 40 miles of driving on one fill of the generator. This car survived the war and is displayed at auto shows worldwide. (From the author's collection.)

The "Rolland" trailer-mounted gazogene. One truly ingenious application was the "Gazogene sur Remorque," a unit designed to attach to a vehicle or as a free-standing source of wood gas. (From the author's collection.)

Trailer (derriere), "pusher" (avant), or free-standing. Attached to a vehicle, the trailer unit provided wood gas to the carburetor via a conducting tube. The ad states that the unit could be hooked up in five minutes, so there must have been a "quick-connect" provided for this feature. In addition, one could purchase a stationary motor which could be attached to the gas-producing trailer to run equipment like generators, pumps, or even a wine press. This auxiliary power unit (upper left, lower right) appears to be crank started. (From the author's collection)

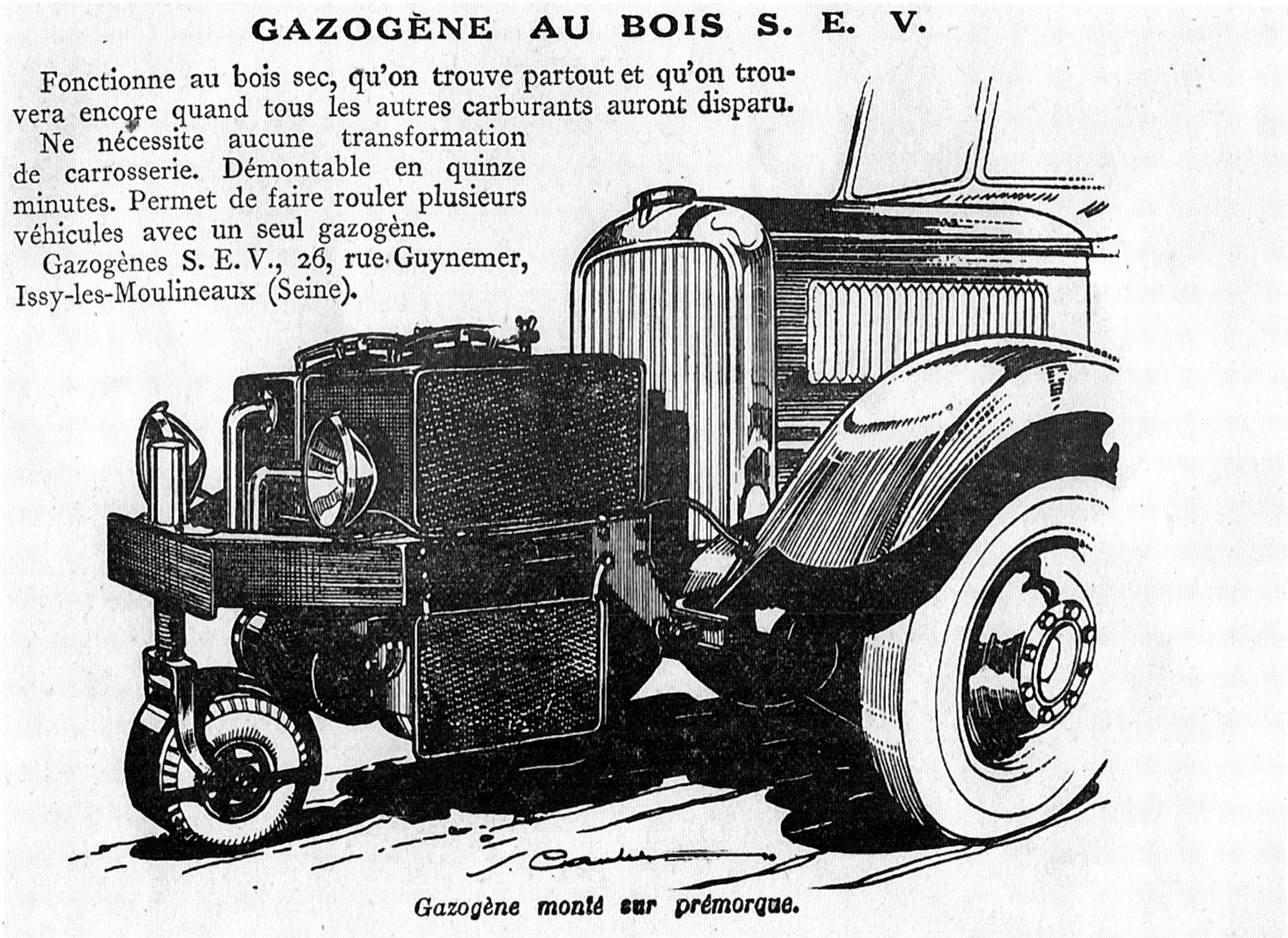

Advertisement for a "premorque," or "pusher" gas generator published in a Paris newspaper 13 September 1941. The ad says the unit can be hooked up in 15 minutes. One distinct advantage of this approach is that the generator can be attached to different vehicles providing they have the connection assembly in place. The headlights built into the generator assembly are a very practical touch. (From the author's collection.)

As seen, the unit could also be mounted ***in front*** of a vehicle, to allow pulling of a different trailer or to preserve easy cargo access for a truck. The attachment was a rigid, two-point connector, and the trailer had but a single wheel so the "remorque" did not wobble. A schematic below shows how these trailer units worked.

In England, rationing also denied fuel to ordinary folk, so a number of strategies were applied. Much more common in England than France was the use of a coal-fired gas producer.

As in France, trailers were employed in Britain.

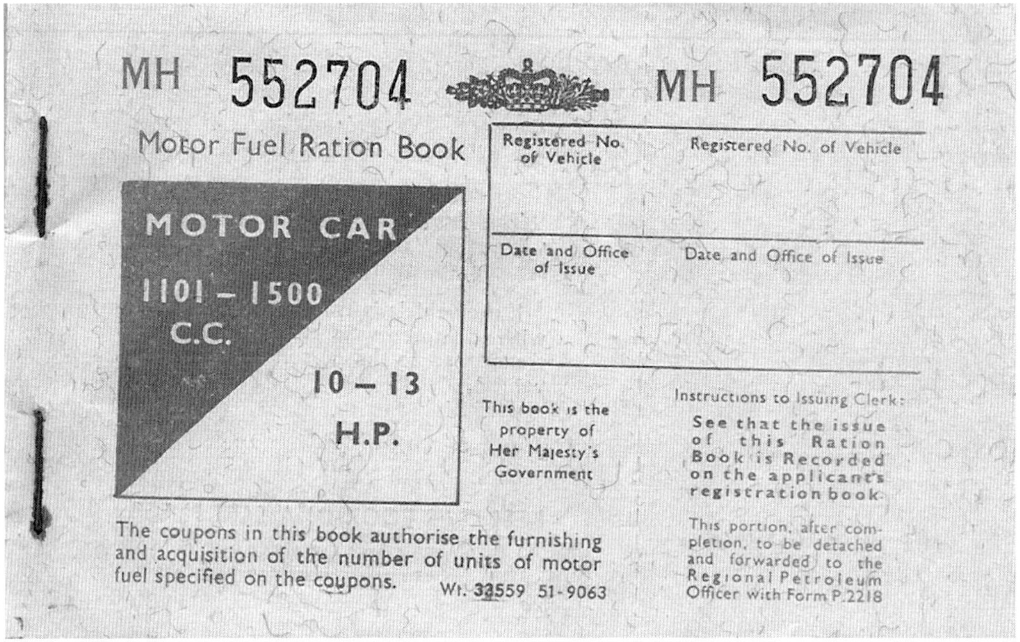

MH 552704 MH 552704

Motor Fuel Ration Book

MOTOR CAR

1101 – 1500 C.C.

10 – 13 H.P.

Registered No. of Vehicle

Registered No. of Vehicle

Date and Office of Issue

Date and Office of Issue

This book is the property of Her Majesty's Government

Instructions to Issuing Clerk: See that the issue of this Ration Book is Recorded on the applicant's registration book.

This portion, after completion, to be detached and forwarded to the Regional Petroleum Officer with Form P.2218

The coupons in this book authorise the furnishing and acquisition of the number of units of motor fuel specified on the coupons. Wt. 32559 51-9063

British ration book. (From the author's collection.)

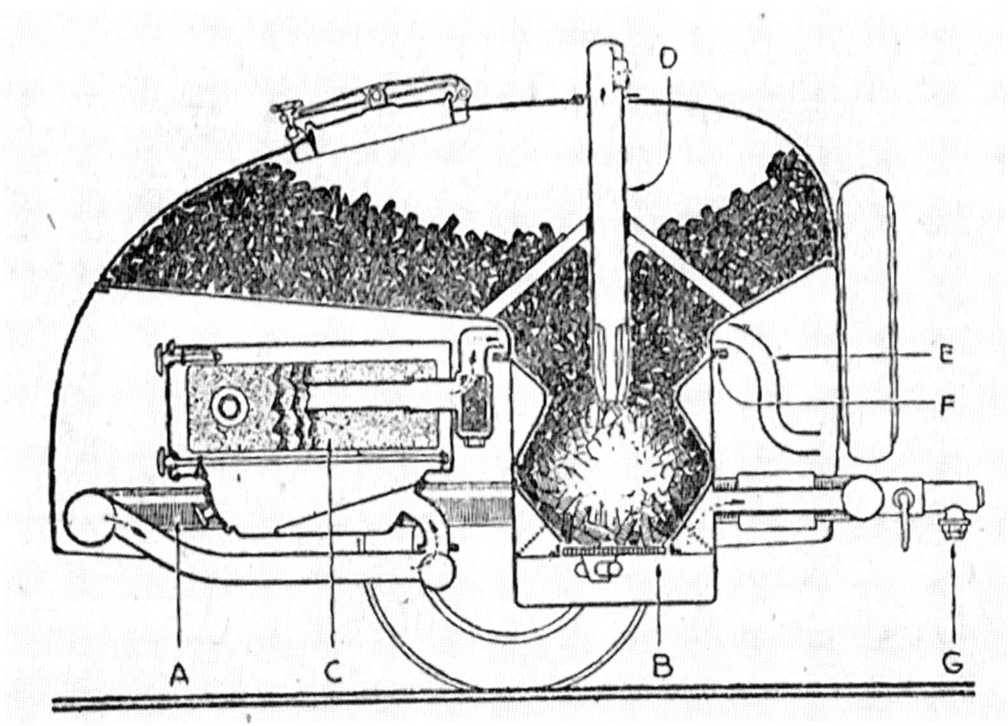

This drawing is a schematic of another "remorque/premorque" (trailer/pusher) manufactured by Panhard. Again, the fundamental elements are present: A. Cooling tubes, B. burner or firebox, C. Filter, D. Air vents, E. Tube conducting gas to motor, F. Pressure relief valve (?), and G. Trailer hitch to vehicle. The sealed fuel-loading hatch is at the top. (From the author's collection.)

Designed & composed in America.
Printed in China.

Coal is added to the firebox at the direction of the lady of the house. The caption of the original points out that the vehicle can be reconverted to liquid fuel "with the turn of a tap"—presumably after the war. (Reprint permission courtesy of the British Science Museum)

The use of solid fuel gas converters for public transportation is a practical application of gas-producers, as the vehicles run constantly, operate at low speed, and are always in range of a refueling station.

Less practical perhaps is this application of a coal burner to a fire engine. Unless the burner was kept "cooking," which increased fuel consumption, the response time for these units must have been woeful. Perhaps the unit was designed to be in reserve, "fired up" as soon as major air raids were predicted for its response area, and then was able to respond promptly when summoned. Of course, once lit, the unit would have to be parked outdoors. With water on board in the firefighting tank this would be a problem in winter.

Famous double-decker English bus powered by coal-burning gas producer, Leeds, England, 1943. Note the white paint applied to the rear fenders and towbar, aiding visibility during blackouts. (Reprinted with permission of the Imperial War Museum.)

Officials view a coal-powered fire engine in a wartime newspaper photo. (Reprinted with permission of the International Science and Society picture library.)

After U.S. entry into the war in 1941 fuel rationing was instituted nationwide. In the case of the U.S., rationing was aimed not so much at conserving fuel, which was available from domestic fields, but to save rubber. With the Japanese occupying or threatening Malaya and the Dutch colonies rubber was scarce, and tires were very difficult to obtain. Many American vehicles spent the war jacked up on blocks due to the unavailability of tires. Rationing fuel restricted unnecessary driving, as cars which were driven less consumed less rubber. Rubber recycling programs collected old tires, rubber balls, and old rainwear.

New cars were also nearly impossible to obtain. In the war years (1941-1945) only 139 new cars were manufactured in the U.S., many of those going to the armed forces. Despite rationing, Americans largely did not resort to alternative fuels, and none of the European improvisations like gas producer vehicles became common in America. One might say that while obtaining fuel in America was difficult, depending upon one's ration classification, Americans got by. Fuel in America may have been scarce, but in Occupied Europe it was nearly nonexistent. We should also remember that American cities in the '40s were not yet completely redesigned to accommodate the automobile, and public transportation infrastructure was extensive. Neighborhood shops within walking distance of consumers were still common in urban areas. Peer pressure also limited fuel use, encouraged by constant advertisement and exhortation from the government. The phrase "***Is this trip really necessary?***" became a standby in comedy, often uttered by an endlessly falling Bugs Bunny. Patriotic posters emphasized the connection between well-being of the troops and civilian conservation. Yes, there was a time in America when going to war meant more than putting a ribbon decal on one's car.

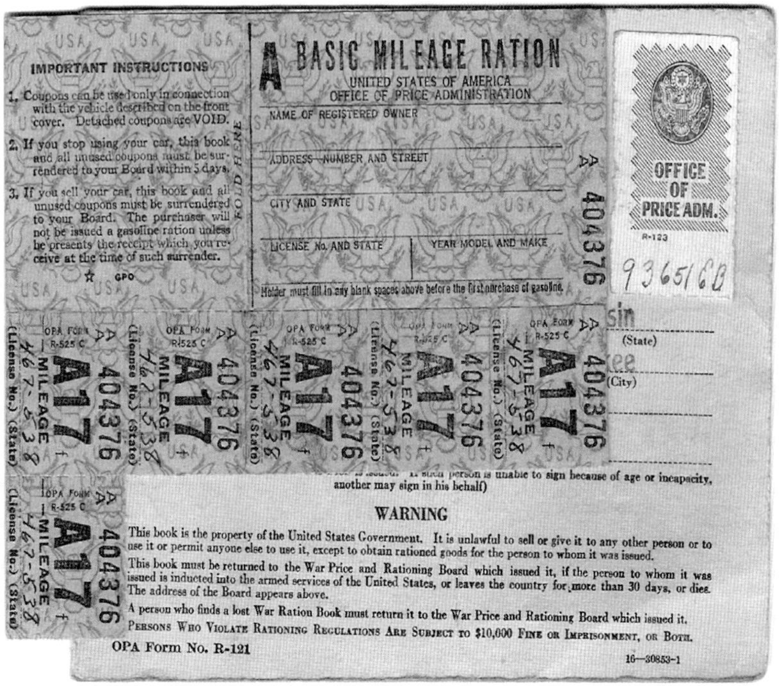

Windshield sticker, patriotic poster stressing rubber conservation, and U.S. ration book with gas stamps. The owner has applied his ration book number to each stamp to prevent theft and black market use.

In Germany, home of the Imbert system, experience with gas producer vehicles was considerable. Immediately after WWI, a "Committee for Technology and Agriculture" was set up to conduct experiments in alternative motor fuels. Indeed, a gas producer bus constructed in collaboration with Herschel and Son operated between Rostock and Warnemunde in the late '20s. The bus used an early model of the Imbert system. The bus had an 80 hp engine, could attain a top speed of 65 km/h, and burned 140 kg of wood fuel per day. While fuel consumption may seem high, one must consider that the bus spent about 50% of its time burning fuel while stopped. In applications like busses and short haul trucks the gas producers were considered popular and efficient, but it was not until the fuel needs of Germany's armed forces began to pinch civilian supplies that *holzgas* vehicles became essential to the economy.

In 1940, Adolf Hitler himself advocated the use of such vehicles during a visit to a Mercedes demonstration.

On this occasion Hitler endorsed development of these vehicles, saying in part:

"Vehicles of this sort will also hold a special place after the war. With increasing motorization we will not be so dependent upon liquid, therefore imported fuel. This will benefit our own economic system" (Quoted in "Generator Jahrbook, 1942," Kasper and Co. Berlin, 1942)

This, other governmental incentives, and increasing liquid fuel shortages prompted rapid adoption of gas producer vehicles and expansion of the infrastructure which supported them.

Fuel production became rationalized, wood fuel falling under the Chief Forest Master's office. Fuel production was contracted out to various business interests, who advertised, sold stock, and competed with one another within the limits of the Reich's economic blueprint, the successive four-year plans. Production was also regulated by the armed forces, and local provincial agencies. The governmental subunits ("Lander") controlled mining, turf-cutting, and so forth.

Wood-powered bus. The apparatus is mounted at the rear. (From the author's collection.)

On July 15, 1940, Hitler attends a Mercedes-Benz demonstration of alternative fuel vehicles. Next to him is Mercedes director Dr. Werdlin, per the original caption.

One typical company was Runo-Everth, based in Munich and Vienna. Runo-Everth provided "All things required for vehicles and stationary installations" using "Generator Wood, Generator Peat (turf), Generator Charcoal and Generator Coal." The company also provided lubricating oil, and had established distribution points throughout Bavaria and Austria, according to its advertising. "Tankholzstelle" (Wood fuel points) were located throughout the country, usually associated with pre-existing gasoline stations.

Far right: 1000 Reichsmarks share in "Generatorkraft," a fuel supplier. Note bottom left the signature of a Lieutenant Colonel in the *Oberkommando des Heeres* (OKH), the central military authority, which also regulated production. (From author's collection.)

AKTIE

Nr. 001457 *

Der/Die

vom Hagen & Sohn

Schwelm

ist bei der

Generatorkraft
Aktiengesellschaft für Tankholz
und andere Generatorkraftstoffe

in Berlin mit

1000 Reichsmark
(Eintausend Reichsmark)

auf das in Aktien zerlegte Grundkapital der Gesellschaft von 1 829 000 Reichsmark beteiligt.

Zur Übertragung dieser Aktie ist gemäß § 3 Abs. 1 der Satzung die Genehmigung der Hauptversammlung durch Mehrheitsbeschluß erforderlich.

Berlin, den 8. Oktober 1941

Der Aufsichtsrat:

Oberstleutnant i. OKH.

Der Vorstand:

In addition to major industrial producers, some fuels were amenable to local "cottage industry" production, primarily wood fuel. Large and small machines were produced for wood fuel manufacture. The machines were designed to reduce raw wood to roughly cylindrical "pellets" no more than 8 cm long and 3-5 cm in diameter. Imagine an oversized wooden thread spool for an approximation of an individual fuel unit. Therefore, the machines had to debark, grind, and cut raw wood to the appropriate size and shape.

Advertisement for a "Gasoholz-Schnitzel" capable of handling wood up to 14 cm in diameter. (From the author's collection.)

Small-scale local production of "tankholz" using small limbs discarded from other forestry operations. Note the size and shape of the product. (From the author's collection.)

The primary difference between machines seems to have been the diameter of raw wood that each would accept. Ideally, the wood products utilized would be "abfallholz," or waste wood. This could be wood left over from production of such things as telephone poles, railroad sleepers, and other large shaped wood products, or waste wood gathered in forestry operations, like branches and limbs. Such distribution was overseen by local forest masters, who located and allocated such resources.

After forming, the wood had to be dried, either in an oven, or by being stored over winter. Obviously the ideal wood source for production was pre dried wood. The proper shape of wood fuel was required so that the fuel would feed evenly to the burning chamber, avoiding "bridging" or blockage of fuel flow by partially burned balks of fuel.

Large scale, mobile production machines. Note the diameter of raw wood stacked to the side of the machine on the right. (From the author's collection.)

With adequate infrastructure in place, German use of "holzvergaser" vehicles increased rapidly during the war years. Major vehicle manufacturers like Opel, VW, GM, Ford, Bussing, Damlier-Benz, M.A.N., and others all began to produce woodburning vehicles, both for the civilian market and the German armed forces.

Seen here is the VW Type 82 factory modified with a woodburner. The bottom of the burner (seen beneath the front bumper) limits the unit's ground clearance. Since the woodburning unit occupies the storage area under the hood, the spare tire has had to be moved to the roof rack, which of course also accommodates the bags of fuel. The gas filter or cooler can be seen below the passenger door. The "hand-hammered" appearance of the bulbous hood indicates that this is probably an early pre-production prototype.

The type 82 VW was designed for military use, having a higher ground clearance than the original KdF Volkswagen. The vehicle was intended as a liason vehicle and to transport (usually junior) officers. (Reprinted with permission VW AG, Wolfsburg, Germany.)

Seen below is what is probably the most recognizable of German woodburners, the light 4X2 *Personenkraftwagen* K1 type 82, another VW variant designed exclusively for the military. These vehicles were among those referred to by the Germans as "kubelwagen." Once again it can be seen that the installation interferes with the unit's ground clearance, which limits its military use. This vehicle has frequently been reproduced as a plastic model.

(Reprinted with permission VW AG, Wolfsburg, Germany.)

By 1942, *Holzvergaser* were common enough that cartoons could be published in newspapers about their use. This example is redrawn from an original published in the "Berlin Morgenpost" October 9, 1942.

„Da staunste, was? Brate mir 'n paar Kartoffeln auf dem Generator, bis der Alte kommt"

"Pretty clever, eh? I'm frying up a couple of potatoes on the Generator before the Boss comes." (From the author's collection.)

Similar truck to that shown in the preceding cartoon. A new door has been created in the side of the van body so that the generator does not interfere with cargo loading. (From the author's collection.)

Even motorcycles were adapted to gas generators. This is a 1937 model from Belgium, capable of over 60 mph burning wood or 72 mph using gasoline. The unit is described as "clumsy" due to the retrofitted burner at the rear. (From the author's collection.)

One of the most practical and successful applications of the wood-fuel concept was their employment in agricultural tractors.

Germany had experienced terrible famine during WWI due to the over-commitment of domestic horsepower to the armed forces, reducing tractive power available for farming and thus multiplying the effect of the Allied blockade. By WWII wood-powered tractors were operating all over Germany. Operating in limited-mileage applications and close to rural fuel sources, these units were so efficient that their use continued into the '60s. The U.S. Federal Emergency Management Agency published a pamphlet in the '80s describing design and use of wood-powered tractors for use in a "national emergency," presumably a catastrophic absence of fuel.

Advertisement for the Lanz L-25 tractor with *holzgas* engine. The tractor could operate for 4-5 hours with one filling (60 kg) of "tankholz." On a firm, flat, dry surface, the ad claims, the unit could pull 22 metric tons in first gear. (From the author's collection.)

Other tractors like the Lanz Bulldog, the Fahr Holzgasschlepper HG 25, and the heavy FAMO Gas Raupenschlepper (caterpillar tractor) were used to try to maintain German agricultural production despite severe shortages of liquid fuel and draft horses.

(From the author's collection.)

(From the author's collection.)

Automakers throughout Germany produced gas generator vehicles.

Damlier-Benz 170 (*vergaser*) produced 1939-1943, with gas-producer schematic (next page). This smart-looking car could reach 80 km/hour, and had a fuel capacity of 15 kg of wood, developing 22 horsepower at 2300 rpm. It weighed 1600 kg, was 4550 mm in length, 1570 mm wide, and had a turning circle diameter of 11 meters. The power plant is an Imbert-style *holzvergaser* manufactured by Damlier-Benz as the model G 136. The specification sheet indicates that the gas-generator system is also available to be installed in existing vehicles, and that the generator cost RM1000. (Reprinted with permission of Daimler-Chrysler, GmbH.)

Schematic showing gas producer and piping. (Reprinted with permission of Daimler-Chrysler, GmbH.)

GM
GENERAL MOTORS

Superb GM Limousine marketed in Denmark. The vehicle is factory built, as demonstrated by the neat application of the woodburner. Note the blackout headlights. In actual use the vehicle would probably have had a roof rack for fuel storage. (From the author's collection.)

GM
GENERAL MOTORS

Such elegant vehicles were in great demand by officials of the Third Reich. (From the author's collection.)

Mercedes advertisement for a Type 230 sedan with trunk-mounted gas generator, 1942. (From the author's collection.)

Another Mercedes Type 230 parked on a street in occupied Poland in 1942. A uniformed German soldier approaches from the left. The car may have used gasoline at least some of the time, as a German military gas can is wedged behind the spare tire on the front fender. Like the GM limousine, luxurious vehicles of this sort would most likely be restricted to high party officials, diplomats, ranking officers, or other elites. (From the author's collection.)

With the war going badly for Germany, it became obvious to economic planners that the great automotive need in Germany and her conquered territories was for trucks, not personal cars. Moreover, those trucks had to use alternative fuels.

First, huge losses in vehicles had occurred during the terrible Russian winters. Second, the heavy European draft horses needed by the *Wehrmacht* to move supplies had died by the thousands during the eastern campaigns due to cold, malnutrition, and overwork. The big European breeds could simply not adapt to the climate and poor roads. Third, the rail system in the Soviet Union could simply not be adapted rapidly enough to Western European gauge, and locomotives were in short supply. Therefore, supplies for troops had to be ferried from distant railheads to the front by truck, and trucks were in short supply, as was fuel. The troops improvised as best they could, using scrawny native Russian *panje* horses to carry small loads on sleds or light carts, but the lack of trucks (and, of course, fuel) became acute.

Factories began to gear up to produce huge quantities of wood or coal-burning trucks. Despite lack of raw materials, allied bombing, and desperate shortages of labor and other handicaps, the industries of Germany and Occupied Europe struggled to meet the demand.

An advertisement, from the Büssing firm in Braunschweig, portrays an endless column of husky super heavy woodburning trucks. Given the enormous difficulties faced by German industry, this would at first glance seem wishful thinking, but in 1943, the German firm M.A.N. managed to produce 3,000 4.5 Ton *holzvergaser* trucks to *Wehrmacht* specifications. Most of these trucks were absorbed by the civilian economy, where they were desperately needed, but others found their way into the German military. By the end of the war, an estimated 100,000 solid-fuel trucks operated in Germany or with the armed forces.

Saurer, an Austrian firm, issued the advertisement shown here. An unconscious irony is the small horsedrawn wagon in the background, which eerily resembles a Russian *panje* cart.

M.A.N. production line, 1943.

Trucks in column.

Opel advertisement.

Opel manufactured this brand new "Blitz" 3-ton woodburner in 1941. It is destined for the military, as evidenced by the helmet-shaped "tarnscheinwerfer" mounted forward on the driver's side fender. One wonders what became of this pristine truck. (Reprinted with permission of Adam Opel AG Historical Archives.)

Another group of Opel "Blitz" 3-ton trucks "mit Imbert holzgasanlage" circa 1941. The small apparatus on the driver's side fender seems to be a warning bell. (Reprinted with permission of Adam Opel AG Historical Archives.)

This 1942 advertisement is for a coal-burning unit.

Mercedes Truck with "Schlafkabine" (sleeper) behind the driver's compartment. It must have been warm, because the boiler is also mounted behind the cab. (From the author's collection.)

Mercedes also contributed woodburning trucks. This rugged L 4500 "tipper" (dump truck) was manufactured in 1942. (Reprinted with permission of Daimler-Chrysler, GmbH.)

Same truck with other side view, showing firebox or boiler. Most German military vehicles listed the preferred tire pressure in white paint on the fender above the tire. The small exhaust pipe projecting in front of the muffler next to the firebox is the "test pipe" used to check fuel ignition before starting. See the appendix for operator directions. (Reprinted with permission of Daimler-Chrysler, GmbH.)

At the risk of redundancy, and so as not to waste a beautiful photo, the same "tipper" truck, tipped. The woodburner apparatus does not interfere with the function of the bed. (Reprinted with permission of Daimler-Chrysler, GmbH.)

Ford advertisement. (From the author's collection.)

Ford pickup. (From the author's collection.)

Ford Van. Note side door. (From the author's collection.)

In addition to the drive to produce as many alternative fuel vehicles as possible, government pressure was applied to encourage owners of vehicles to convert them to other fuels. In 1942 Albert Speer, then in charge of armaments, issued the following directive:

Excerpts from German government decree regarding vehicle conversion.

"Each vehicle owner who is aware of his responsibility to the transportation sector of the economy must convert his commercial vehicle to operation with generator gas. Generators and conversion parts will be supplied in sufficient quantity. The turning on of private initiative and of personal responsibility of entrepreneurs has made possible immense increase in production in the German armaments industry. *I expect that the owners of commercial vehicles step up to the plate in the same way as the armaments industry did and take on the conversion of their commercial vehicles on their own responsibility* (emphasis added). In agreement with the Reichsminister of the Economy I have directed the following decree to the Central Office for Generators:

1. Owners of *bewinkelte** commercial vehicles (excepting emergency/temporary delivery vehicles) who are in the position to convert their vehicles to gas generator or high or low density/pressure gas operation without having to resort to making use of others' workshops will receive the necessary permission from the relevant authorities if they apply and in contrast to the generally applicable rules.

2. Conversions carried out under the initiative of vehicle owners will also be eligible for a non-redeemable subsidy of respectively 1000 Reichsmark for vehicles with diesel motors and 600 Reichsmark for vehicles with carburetors. For conversion of vehicles with dual fuel operation (diesel-gas process) to single fuel operation this subsidy will be 400 Reichsmark.

3. Vehicle owners who have converted commercial vehicles (excepting emergency/temporary delivery vehicles) in their own workshops to gas generator or high or low density/pressure gas operation will be favored in the granting of exemptions for the conversion of automobiles or emergency/temporary delivery vehicles, if the conversion takes place in their own workshops and the use of the automobile or emergency/temporary delivery vehicle lies within the framework of applicable regulations concerning *Bewinkelung*. Generators suitable for the conversion of automobiles will be distributed by the Central Office for Generators by those responsible for local transport.

I hereby urge all vehicle owners to undertake conversion on their own responsibility and to register with the local traffic authority as agents of the Central Office for generators (emphasis in the original).

The representatives of the central office will direct to the vehicle owners the generators and motor conversion parts that are to be installed, offer expert advice' and after successful conversion will pay the government subsidy. After the conversion of commercial vehicles they will give out permits for the conversion of automobiles."

Reichsminister Albert Speer, October 1942.

German bureaucratic language is very dense. In essence this statement called upon commercial vehicle owners to convert vehicles with a subsidy, and promises leniency regarding conversion of automobiles to those who can convert their commercial vehicles in their own shops. The tone of the message is that vehicle owners are *strongly* encouraged to convert, and that conversion is a matter of urgency.

Appeals and directives of this sort, emphasizing compliance as a matter of national duty, had great authority in National Socialist Germany. Failure to comply was felt to imply lack of patriotism.

* The term "bewinkelte" is very obscure, but in this context appears to mean "specially designated," as in the phrase "vehicles specially designated for national service." Vehicles could be "rot bewinkelt" (designated in red), a term used in a Berlin wartime document concerning transport. In that application, a red "V" was applied to the license plate and the vehicle's papers. "Bewinklung" refers to the state of being specially designated, for which the vehicle's use had to meet certain requirements, like delivering mail. These vehicles may have been exempt from conversion, or qualified for special reimbursement.

An alternative fuel truck (Büssing-NAG?) makes a delivery...

...To an important customer. The symbol near the doorway designates a political organization of the NSDAP, the Nazi party.

License plate with "Winkel." Usually this "V" shape was in red.

Holzvergasers at War

The drain of Germany's resources to the Eastern Front affected all aspects of life, both civilian and military. As vehicles were destroyed, lost, or mechanically worn out, more and more replacements were summoned from domestic German sources and quieter military areas. Liquid fuel was also allocated mainly to the east, so both military and civilian mobility in the rest of the continent came to depend on wood gas and other biomass fuels. Even combat units accommodated alternative fuel vehicles as support transport. The handbook at right is a maintenance and training manual for the Opel 3-ton Blitz truck, and it is stamped as belonging to the "Command of the Assault gun School" in Military District 5.

There are persistent rumors that even tanks were powered by woodburners. Research reveals little evidence for this, except that there is some indication that a few older tanks, stripped of armor and powered by *holzvergaser*, were used for driver training.

Consider the fuel consumption of a tank. Even a light tank, like the early-war PzKW II, consumed 1.1 L of fuel/km. Therefore, to have a range of 100 km, a tank would have had to carry 110 kg (242 lb) of bulky wood fuel. Also, the piping and so forth would have to be outside the tank due to the danger of CO, and the tank would thus be vulnerable to damage from even light infantry weapons.

A super-heavy tank, like the Tiger, burned 5 liters of fuel *per kilometer*. To imagine such a vehicle powered by wood gas is ludicrous.

Extract from the letter of the Supreme Command of the *Wehrmacht* General of Motor Vehicles of Dec. 22, 1942, Main Inst./VIIIv No. 0284/42:

Re: Operational Safety in Operation of Generator-Vehicles.

In Reference to: Publication in HV-Blatt, 24 Year, Dec. 11, 1942, Part B, Page 23, No. 925.

The following construction guidelines are to be observed in future in the conversion of Wehrmacht vehicles to operation with generators and the relevant repair shops and service offices are to be informed.

For all vehicles of the Wehrmacht the regulations are to be followed as laid out in the above-referenced publication under the rubric A "General technical safety set-up of generator vehicles."

Service manual with military stamp.

Further, for all vehicles that are to be retrofitted for the Wehrmacht, a *Flammendurchschlagssicherung* (a device to prevent flame from emitting from the ignition hole - Ed.) is to be installed over the ignition hole.

Only vehicles of landbased units that because of their type and their use will never be utilized to transport munitions, explosives, flammable liquids and flammable gasses are to be excepted from the further construction regulations under Points B "Transport of munitions and Explosives" and C "Transport of flammable liquids and flammable gasses.

The construction regulations under Point D "Transport of roughage and other easily flammable substances" only apply to vehicles that are habitually used for this purpose. If in doubt, these rules apply.

Flammendurchschlagssicherungen are those that prevent the escape of a naked flame from the generator through the ignition hole (for example, a close woven metal cloth such as is used in mining lamps, labyrinthine metal ring fillers or the like).

For the heat insulating dividing wall (transport of munitions and explosives) use may be made of material such as for example asbestos cardboard, a double sheet metal wall with interior airfilled space, or the like.

For the Head of the Supreme Command of the Wehrmacht

Signed: Paulus

This is the face sheet of a series of orders regulating use of *holzvergaser* by the *Wehrmacht*. The remainder of this document prescribes a great many details like convoy spacing, operation in munitions facilities, and safety regarding Carbon Monoxide and the like.

Note the signature, Friederich Paulus. Paulus was heavily engaged as commander of the German VI army at Stalingrad in December 1942, but this document was prepared under his supervision prior to that assignment; thus, it still bears his signature at the date of its publication. Paulus' assignment prior to his command of VI army was Deputy Chief of Staff of the Army (1A). Paulus was to surrender to the Soviets in January 1943. After his surrender, the Soviets consistently referred to him as "*von* Paulus," but this is inaccurate, as Paulus was not an aristocrat.

Wehrmacht specifications for *holzvergaser* required that a space or shield be present between the gas generator and finely divided flammables like hay or straw. Installing a shield allowed compliance without requiring major alterations of the truck bed. This civilian truck has a tall shield for high loads and a ladder for filling the generator. (From the author's collection.)

Tatra military truck with a shorter shield. (From the author's collection.)

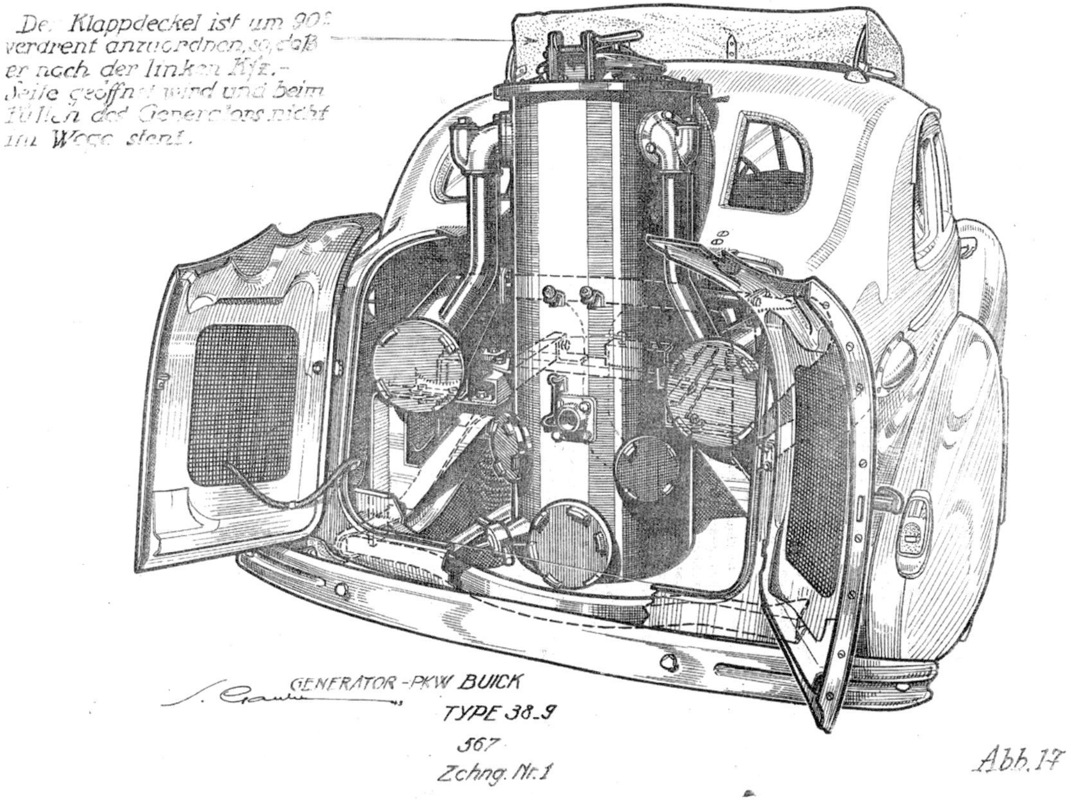

A meticulous drawing of a woodburner installation in a Buick auto. This detailed schematic is part of a *Wehrmacht* document listing specifications and recommendations for military use of *holzvergaser* vehicles. The legend specifies the placement of the sealing apparatus so that the firebox can be easily filled.

Luftwaffe soldiers are photographed in front of a "requisitioned" French Renault "gazogene" truck. (From the author's collection.)

A military class gathers around as the instructor explains the operation of a *holzvergaser*. The truck is almost certainly a cab-over-engine Renault. The canvas top of the cargo area seems to be modified to accommodate the firebox piping. What is the German for "Listen up, Maggot!?" (Courtesy the Daniel Hagen Collection.)

Young soldiers line up in front of a 3-ton Mercedes coal burner. The troops are wearing late-war leather-conserving gaiters, or "gamaschen," and reissued tunics of the 1936 type. Since the soldiers have no rank or decorations, and because of their youth, the impression is that these are late-war trainees. (From the author's collection.)

German soldiers loved to pose with their "steeds." The archives are full of pictures of soldiers standing proudly next to their trucks. For one thing, driving a heavy truck accorded considerable status in a country where most people did not drive, a country where only one person in 52 had a motor vehicle. These two soldiers are posing with their heavy Mercedes *holzvergaser*-trailer combination. The vehicle bears "WH" plates, identifying it as an army vehicle, probably from the Breslau military district, and the parallel-stripe markings on the right fender designate a transportation unit. The vehicle is painted in the standard post-1943 yellow-tan color. The blackout lamp is unusual, and may be a British item captured earlier in the war. (From the author's collection.)

German troops surround an overturned wood-powered bus in Norway. The troops are wearing reed-green "drillich" fatigue uniforms, are unarmed, and thus are almost certainly a work detail. They seem delighted to have survived the crash, and also are probably happy that their detail is now postponed. In this photo, the censor appears to have scratched out an armband on the soldier in the middle near foreground. The man might be wearing a traffic-control armband, which could identify his unit. (From the author's collection.)

The bus appears to be a conversion, rather than a factory-produced vehicle. (From the author's collection.)

A *Wehrmacht* armored personnel carrier type 251 sits on a street in a Scandinavian town. The woodburning conversion is very complex and cumbersome. For one thing, the installation blocks the rear door through which troops enter or exit. The firebox is at the rear, and the round appliances on the sides of the firebox near the top may be centrifugal filters. The gas is piped from these units into the long cylinders along the sides of the vehicle, which are also filters. From these filters the gas is piped to a cylindrical cooler/filter at the front of the vehicle, then through the armored hood to the engine. (From the author's collection.)

This photo shows the front of the same kind of vehicle shown on the preceding page. This view shows the tubes leading from the cylindrical filters along the vehicle's side to the drum-like cooler/filter at the front. From the round cooler/filter, a pipe runs through the armored hood to the engine. It may be that one of the vehicles has broken down and the other is preparing to tow it away. With all the thin, vulnerable piping and high silhouette, these 251s are obviously not meant for combat. These vehicles are either stopgap heavy transport and recovery vehicles or, more likely, driver training units. (From the author's collection.)

At the Dnepr River, a damaged high bridge has been restored by German forces. A column of men, probably POWs (one is wearing a standard Soviet backpack, another a military cap, and all are wearing military greatcoats), carries crates to the opposite bank. In the middle of the bridge is a Soviet ZIS 21 truck with a gas generator. Because of the exposure, it is impossible to tell whether the truck is operated by German personnel or Soviet civilians.

Nur für den Dienstgebrauch!

Prop.-Kp. Lw 5 Archiv-Nr.: 1327/19

Bildberichter: v. Kaler Text: Scharkowski

Ort: Dnjepropetrowsk Datum: 8.11.41.

Text:

Wiederhergestellte Hochbrücke über den Dnjepr, die den Namen "Kleistbrücke" erhielt.

Zensurvermerk mit Angabe der Gründe:

Original photo tag indicates that this photo was taken by a *Luftwaffe* "kriegsberichter" (war reporter) on November 11, 1941. The tag says that the restored bridge has been named the Kleist bridge, after Field Marshall von Kleist. The city may be Dnepropetrovsk.

Unidentified *Wehrmacht* truck prepared for a long winter's night. To protect the oil pan from the weather, all sorts of objects, including the driver's seat, are stacked around the lower engine. This vehicle is equipped with an external gas burner, the muffler-like assembly on the driver's side fender. In the foreground is a kit of tubing and so forth to allow the heat from that burner to be used to warm other vehicles. (From the author's collection.)

The "heissluftbläser"(hot air blower) was an innovative use of the woodburner's products. The unit was used to warm up other vehicles prior to starting them. The gases from the firebox are piped into the muffler-like housing "a" and ignited at the ignition hole "b." A glow-plug, "c," powered by the vehicle's battery, maintains the flame. Hot gas is then carried away via the outlet pipe "d," to which a hose is connected. The hose can be attached to a nozzle, called a "heisspistole," and the heat then directed to the frozen vehicles' oil pan, radiator, etc.

Another hot air blower, "a," mounted on the fender of a truck is being connected to a specially-constructed port in order to warm up its own radiator and filter/cooler unit, "b." The truck carries unit identification for a *Luftwaffe* unit, *Kampfgeschwader* 30, which operated Ju. 88 bombers.

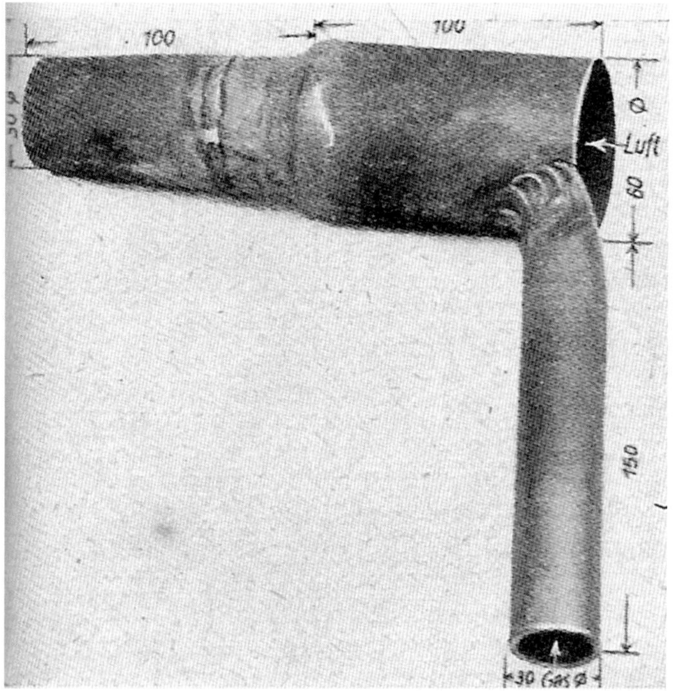

The "Heisspistole" is a locally-produced expedient, thus technical manuals were published which included its design specifications for use by shops in the field. The device operates using the venturi principle. Hot gas is introduced from below, which draws in ambient air, increasing total flow.

Underpan heater was placed beneath the oilpan, and heat applied either with a blowtorch or heat from a woodburner. The heater has adjustable legs to control the distance between the heat source and the oilpan. The army "WH" prefix can still be seen despite the censor's crayon.

"Heisspistole" in use, heating the filter/cooler of an Imbert *holzvergaser*. The heater could be employed either on the vehicle, making its own heating gas, or on other vehicles. An oddity in this handbook is the hit-and-miss manual obscuring of license plate prefixes, probably by a sleepy wartime censor.

Women braiding straw for insulation.

The components of the cooling/filtering system are wrapped in braided straw to protect against the cold. Since the water in the system served not only as a filter and cooler but as a checkvalve against backflow of gas, it could not function when frozen.

Detail of braiding process. "Just like a hairdo" says the caption in the original.

Rugged Mercedes unit equipped for field use. The truck bears the "WL" (*Wehrmacht Luftwaffe*) designation, indicating air force assignment. The folded-down triangular element on the top of the cab is for designating when the vehicle is towing a trailer. The truck appears to be painted in early-war blue grey. (From the author's collection.)

Soldiers pose with a Krupp *holzvergaser* and "The Sweetheart of the Regiment." It was standard practice to stencil the shipping characteristics of a vehicle (empty weight, etc.) on the doors of vehicles.

A military truck clears a checkpoint. Given the gas cooler on the front this is obviously a *holzvergaser*, but not much else can be determined from this photo. The picture is labeled "Citroen with Estonian Volunteers, Pskov, 1942." The truck has an unreadable military unit marking on the driver's side fender and a painted license number on the left front bumper. The soldier nearest the door to the guard shack appears to be wearing a *Feldpolizei gorget*, which was suspended around the neck from chains. From this "badge" the military field police got the nickname "Kettenhund," or "chain dogs," not a term of endearment. (Courtesy the Daniel Hagen Collection.)

Nurses watch as German sailors board a flatbed truck. The men are wearing *Kriegsmarine* caps and captured British battle dress. The man 4th from right is wearing the classic "Donald Duck" naval hat, and the man sitting at the rear of the cab is wearing a unit pin on the side of his cap. From this evidence, we can conclude that these men are submariners. Between cruises submariners were treated very well, as they were viewed as national heroes. They are all carrying walking sticks, so they may be going for an excursion. The truck is a post-factory conversion. Note the pipe running across the top of the cab. From the square shape, the gas generator appears to be of the type manufactured by Wisco. (From the author's collection.)

Wehrmacht troops with weapons aboard a M.A.N. (?) truck with a solid fuel generator; their NCO is seated in the driver's compartment. Note the improvised parking brake in front of the rear wheel and the roof rack for fuel. (From the author's collection.)

Two army officers pause for a chat and a smoke while an enlisted man stirs the firebox, preparatory to adding fuel. (Courtesy the Daniel Hagen Collection.)

Refueling is complete, and the sack previously on the roof is now gone. A French Renault truck bearing army plates is to the right. (Courtesy the Daniel Hagen Collection.)

Two troops are beginning the process for restarting a woodburner with wood remaining in the firebox after shutdown. In order to restart the fire, the leftover wood must be stirred with a wooden pole before new fuel is added and the fire reignited. Under magnification, the truck bears "WL" (*Luftwaffe*) license plates, and the eagle stamp applied to the left of the "W" designates the area or command under which the truck is registered. The soldiers wear the early-war off-white fatigue jacket, low-quarter shoes, and shiny belt buckle consistent with *Luftwaffe* uniform practice. The make of the truck is unknown. (From the author's collection.)

Opel/Mercedes L 701 3-ton in military configuration. The driver's compartment is the "einheitscabine," a standardized cab made partly of wood. Trucks built to military specifications were to include this cab to save metal and standardize production. The truck is painted in the mid-to-late war yellow-tan paint scheme. This example is in the museum in Sinsheim. Alongside the truck is a freestanding *holzvergaser* assembly used to demonstrate operating principles. (Sinsheim Museum, Sinsheim Germany)

Many military woodburners suffered the same fate as their gasoline-powered brethren. Here, a soldier scrounges a severely damaged and partially stripped truck for parts. Above his left shoulder the truck's gas generator is knocked askew. (From the author's collection.)

This photo shows the extent of the damage. The *einheitscab* is broken up, and the metal of the firewall is torn away, as is the door panel. The damage seems inconsistent with a road accident, and more likely stems from artillery, strafing, or bombing. (From the author's collection.)

Solid fuel vehicles soldiered on until the end of the war and beyond. Above, Czech internees are preparing to return to Czechoslovakia after the surrender. The truck appears to be a Mercedes, perhaps a coal-powered unit. The exterior pipe running across the top of the cab indicates a conversion. The men are returning from "Labor Concentration Camp Flossenberg" flying the Czech flag. The men appear fit and well-fed, but the photo is dated October 1945, and the surrender was completed in May. Presumably, they have been nourished and rehabilitated during the ensuing months. (From the author's collection.)

Some military halftracks converted to agriculture or other civilian use. This is an alternative fuel vehicle, but it is unknown whether the conversion was made by the military. This vehicle appears to be an early-war Adler with an added homebuilt civilian cab. The gas generator looks like a coal-powered model due to the finned filter/cooler on the driver's side behind the driver's compartment. The fender over the track appears to be cut off to accommodate the added wooden bed. (From the author's collection.)

Demag half-track, possibly a 1-ton D11 model. The driver's compartment looks like a wartime "Einheitscabine" (standard cab) adapted to fit. From the picture one can make an educated guess that the photo is of the immediate postwar timeframe. The vehicles are heavily adapted to non-military use, and vehicles of this sort were not available to civilians during the war. Two of the men in the picture wear military jackets without decorations or rank insignia, and with the *Wehrmacht* eagle removed, as did many demobilized soldiers. They are also wearing M 1943 caps, which tends to preclude prewar dating. The author remembers one such vehicle, a stripped-down Sdkfz 251 halftrack used in forestry which was still clanking about during his service in Germany in the early '60s. (From the author's collection.)

Almost immediately after the war solid-fuel vehicles fell out of use. The inconvenience and the danger associated with these vehicles was too much for drivers as liquid fuel became available. Though solid fuel vehicles continued to be used in parts of Asia and the Soviet east, most western drivers returned to gasoline as soon as they could. One exception was agriculture, where wood and coal-powered tractors and other vehicles labored on until at least the '60s.

A few of the original gas producer vehicles labored on or were maintained as curiosities, but almost all of the rest were retired or reconverted to gasoline.

A 1936 Opel Wanderer with a gas producer continues to operate in 1980. According to "Chemistry in our Time" volume 3, the owner bought the car in 1945 and has logged 90,000 kilometers since.

Occasionally, a hobbyist or specialist will adapt a vehicle to solid fuel power, but their utility remains limited by the same factors that handicapped the original units: Carbon Monoxide, inconvenience, fire hazard, relatively low power, and requirement for specialty fuel.

Despite its shortcomings, if there is a severe fuel emergency in the future, the *holzvergaser* may return...

The FEMA Publication "Simplified Wood Gas Generator for Fueling Internal Combustion Engines in a Petroleum Emergency," first published in March 1989, describes an "open" or "downdraft" system for wood gas production. This system tends to eliminate much of the Carbon Monoxide hazard according to the publication. The system uses readily available materials, like commercial plumbing parts.

FEMA woddburning tractor during field trials. (FEMA photo.)

An Den Gasfahrer
Stehtst Du vor'm
Generator wagen,
Dankest Du wohl mit bangem Zagen,
Dass er Dir nun Sorgen macht,
Doch er tut's nicht, hast Du acht.
Nimm gutes Tankholz, stückig und trocken,
Nicht zu Klein und nicht zu gross die Brocken,
Ob weich, ob hart is nichts so wichtig
Beides gemischt ist sicher richtig.
Dann mach alle Luken dicht,
Sonst kriegst Du Gas ganz sicher nicht,
Weil's gleich verbrennt im Generator,
Und keine Kraft mehr gibt der Motor
Die Dichtungen halt' immer rein,
Schmeir stets mit Graphitöl ein,
Kondenswasser lass zeitig ab,
Denn sonst macht es die Leistung knapp.
Den Rost rüttle vor'm Tanken heftig
Und stoch're nach der Füllung kräftig.
Den Hohlbrand kannst du dadurch meiden
Und sparst dem Motor damit Leiden.
Hast Du an all' das gut gedacht,
Das Fahren Dir auch Freude macht.
Die Luft stell' immer richtig ein,
Das merke gut, dass muss stets sein.
Auch's Schalten darfst Du nicht vergessen
Denn wirklich wäre es vermessen
Zu denken's könn't' auch ohne geh'n
Sofort bleibt Dir der Motor steh'n
Stets denk' beim Generatorfahren
Dass gut Gas vor allem sei.
Dar wird vor Sorgen Dich bewahren
Bei Deiner Holzgasfahrerei

To the Gas vehicle Driver
If you stand before your
Generator vehicle
You'll probably be thankful (i.e. to have it) but with frightened timidity,
That it's causing you worries
But it won't if you pay attention/take care
Use good fuel wood, blocky and dry,
Not too small and the chunks not too big.
It's not that important whether it's soft or hard,
Mixing both is certainly all right.
Then close all the hatches tight,
Otherwise you won't get any gas,
Because it will burn right up in the generator,
And not give any power to the motor.
Always keep the sealing rings clean,
Always lubricate them with graphite,.
Drain off condensed water in a timely way,
For otherwise it will reduce power.
Shake the grate hard before filling the tank,
And poke strongly after filling,
This way you can avoid cavity burns,
And you spare the motor suffering.
If you've thought of everything properly,
Driving will be a joy for you.
Always adjust the air properly
Pay attention to this, it has to be done always.
Also don't forget to shift gears,
It would really be presumptuous to assume,
Things would work without doing this:
Right away the motor will stall.*
Always remember when driving a generator vehicle,
That good gas is the main thing,
That will protect you from worry
When you drive around in a gas (generator) vehicle.

Anonymous

*Because of lower power and torque, gas generator vehicles had to be downshifted earlier than other vehicles.

Appendix

OPERATION AND SERVICE MANUAL

"IMBERT HOLZGAS ANLAGE

IM

3 To OPEL BLITZ

LASTWAGEN"

Partial translation reprinted with permission of Adam Opel, AG Historical Archives

FOR THE WOOD-GAS DRIVER

This book will offer valuable and detailed advice and will introduce him to the special characteristics of using a wood gas engine. The information given will show that any prejudice against this manner of running an engine is unfounded.

Running a wood-gas engine requires:

- **Correct operation**
- **Proper manner of driving**
- **The specified charcoal fuel - or -**
- **Appropriate fuel-wood**
- **Regular maintenance**

For the charcoal, use well-dried pressed beechwood briquettes in the size of a walnut. Non-processed charcoal that is poorly degassed and contains semi-charcoalized wood is inappropriate and will lead to residue build up in the suction channels and the motor itself. If you reuse charcoal that has already been partially processed in the gas-generator, it should be carefully sieved in order to rid it of cinders and especially of incompletely carbonized wood.

As fuel-wood one should if possible use air-dried hardwood with little moisture content. The pieces of wood should not be larger than a box of matches, but also not larger than a fist. Large chunks of wood, rotten and chunky wood, bark or other impurities, or sawdust will cause cavity burns and even clog up the gas-generator and thus disrupt the production of gas. The best fuel is hardwood such as, for example, beech, whereas soft wood should be mixed carefully with hardwood.

CARBON MONOXIDE is contained in wood-gas, there is thus a very high risk of poisoning. When the motor is turned off, always close the wood-gas hand lever, otherwise there will be a backsurge of the wood-gas that continues to develop in the gas-generator into the area under the hood of the vehicle, thence possibly into the driver's compartment. While driving, always maintain good ventilation in the driver's compartment.

Operation, routine and scheduled maintenance, Opel 3-ton truck. Translated from the original.

FILLING GENERATOR

Gaserzeuger völlig ausgeräumt

1

Turn the toggle lever and open the hinged lid

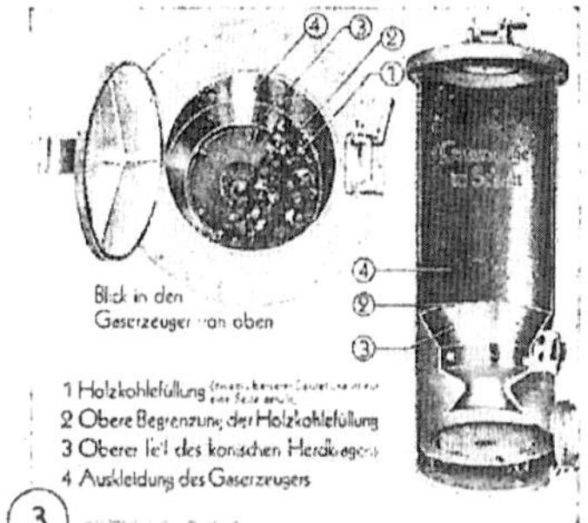

3

...The upper edge of the conical hearth collar

2

Fill the gas generator from above, through the opening to...

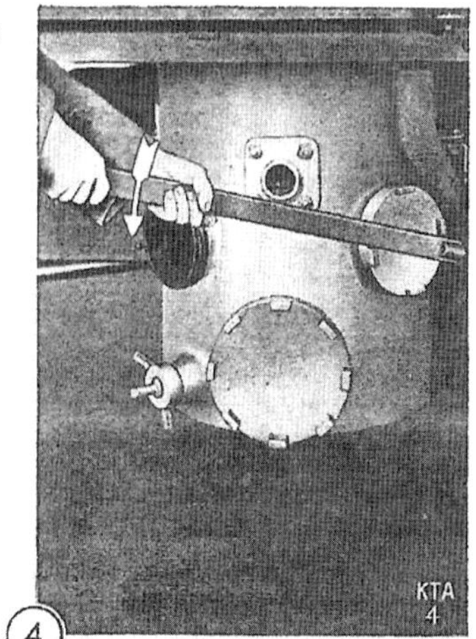

4

Unscrew both hatch covers with the hatch-iron

and on it goes...

5

Fill with wood-fuel or charcoal from outside through the upper hatches

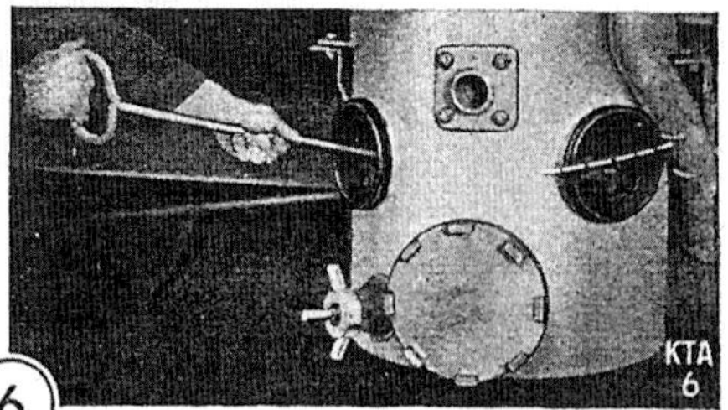

6

With the coal rake, spread the fuel evenly around the hearth supports so that it comes approximately up to the middle of the hatches

7

Turn the threaded cap for the grate pin ("Rutteldorn") about 1/2 turn with the hatch-iron

8

To distribute the fuel, oscillate the grate as well.

9

Tighten the theaded cap for the "grate pin" ("Rutteldorn")

(10)

Brush graphite lubricant onto the two upper hatch covers*

(11)

Screw on all hatch covers and tighten with the hatch iron.

(12)

Fill up the gas-generator all the way from the top with fuel - wood - - never let wood fall between the gas-generator and the external covering - - danger of fire

(13)

Close the hinged cover and turn the toggle lever. Make sure there is no wood lying on the sealing ring. Frequently brush graphite lubricant on the seal of the hinged cover so that it won't stick and be pulled out of it's seat when the lid is opened.

* Any operator can make graphite lubricant himself. Using a metal can, mix old motor oil and stir so that a porridge-like mass arises.

9

Screw on all hatch covers and tighten with the hatch-iron

10

Open the hinged cover. Knock down any wood remnants in the gas-generator with a wooden pole. Be careful not to damage the gas-generator

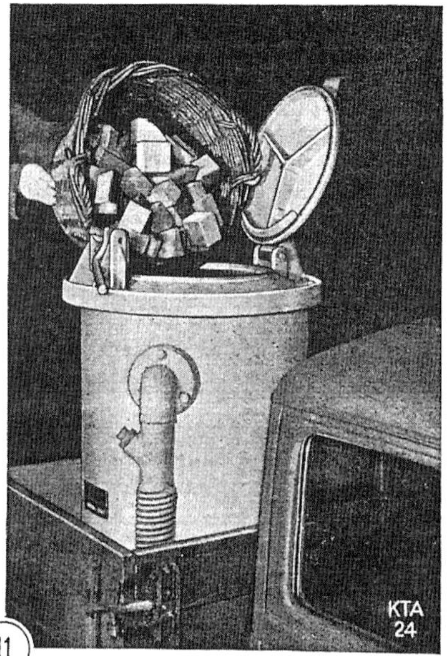

11

Refill fuel-wood into the gas-generator (note the uniform size and shape - Ed.)

12

Close the hinged cover and turn the toggle lever. Make sure there is no wood lying on the sealing ring. Frequently brush graphite lubricant on the seal of the hinged cover so it won't stick and be pulled out of it's seat when the lid is opened.

GASERZEUGER ANZÜNDEN

Lighting the gas-generator

1

Close the air adjustment lever. Pull out the handle for the shut-off flap all he way out. In this way the shut-off flap is opened completely and at the same time the blower is turned on. Let the blower run for at least 1/2 minute in order to suck up any gas remnants that might still be in the gas-generator - Otherwise, there is danger of explosive ignition in the gas-generator.

2

Only after this hold a burning fuse in front of the air-and-ignition hole of the gas generator. Use as a fuse wood-wool or newspaper, never gasoline (danger of explosive ignition.

3

After three or four minutes burning, check the wood gas at the opening of the gas-exhaust pipe to see if it ignites by lighting the stream of gas with a gas lighter or match. The gas should burn with a reddish-blue long flame. If the flame burns at the gas-exhaust pipe opening and doesn't go out...

4

...Then the handle for the shut-off flap should be pushed in all the way. By doing this the shut-off flap is closed completely and the blower is turned off at the same time. The motor must be turned on immediately.

MOTOR ANLASSEN

STARTING THE MOTOR

Before starting check for the required amount of motor oil and coolant levels. The gear shift level must be in neutral

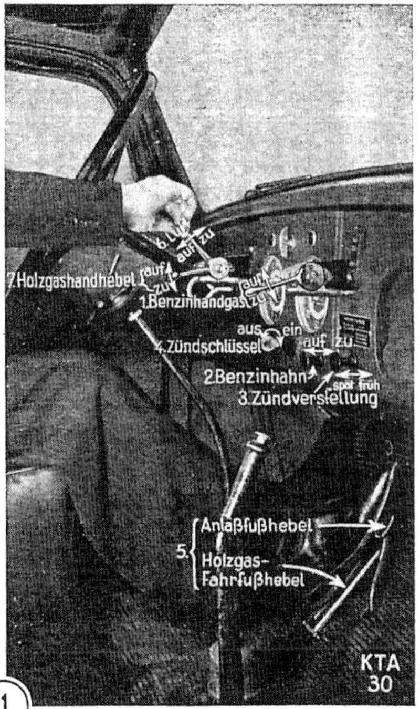

1

To start the motor:

1. The gasoline hand lever (benzinhandgas) should be closed.

2. The button for the gasoline switch (Benzinhahn) should be completely closed. Gasoline is completely shut off.

3. Push in the ignition timing button (Zundeinstellknopf) completely. This corresponds to early ignition.

4. Turn the ignition key (Zundschlussel) to the right - The ignition is turned on.

5. Push down the drive pedal (Fahrfusshebel) all the way and at the same time push down the starting pedal (Anlassfusshebel) all the way.

6. ...and at the same time open up the air adjustment lever (Lufteinstellenhebel) all the way and then close it up to the point that the motor starts.

Release the starting pedal and drive pedal

7. Set the woodgas hand lever (Holzgashandhebel) to neutral and let the motor run.

Shortly after starting the woodgas worsens. In order to get past this so called "weak point" it is necessary to give more gas, if need be full gas and at the same time to close the air adjustment lever a little.

Once this "weak point" is past, the generation of gas corresponds to the position of the drive pedal. THE VEHICLE IS NOW READY TO GO.

STARTING THE MOTOR AND LIGHTING THE GAS-GENERATOR WITH A DAMAGED BLOWER OR WEAK ACCUMULATOR (BATTERY)

Editor's note: Weak batteries were a common problem when these vehicles were used by transport columns in the USSR, as the extreme winter cold quickly sapped battery power.

In this case the motor is started with gasoline. Be careful to fill the gasoline tank ONLY when the woodgas generator is cold.

IMPORTANT: ONLY USE GASOLINE TO START THE MOTOR. Sever damage to the motor, which is carefully sealed for use with woodgas, will be caused by operating with gasoline only or using gasoline in addition to woodgas to increase the output of the motor.

Editor's note:These vehicles could be operated with gasoline exclusively only after modification to the carburetor.

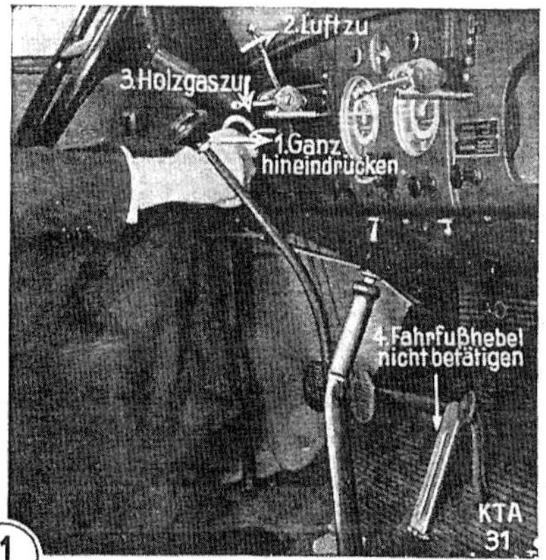

1

For starting the motor:

1. Push in the lever for the shut-off flap (Absperrklappe) all the way - The shut-off flap in the blower duct is now closed.
2. Shut off the air adjustment lever (Lufteinstellhebel) all the way.
3. Shut off the woodgas hand lever (Holzgashandhebel) all the way.
4. Do not push the drive pedal (Fahrfusshebel)

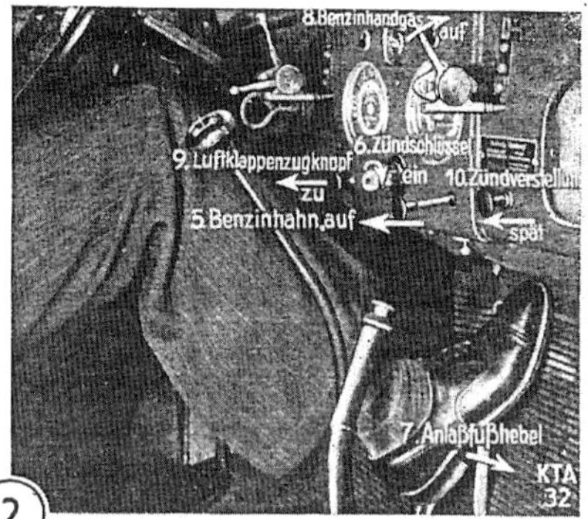

2

5. Pull out the knob for the gasoline switch (Benzinhahn) all the way.

6. Turn the ignition key to the right, ignition is now turned on

7. Depress the starting pedal

8. At the same time give some gas with the gasoline hand level

9. Pull out the air flap knob (Luftklappenzugknopf) with a cold motor and low external temperature in order to make starting up easier*

* **If the motor gets too rich and poorly ignitable gasoline mix because of frequent use of the hand-gas lever and overuse of the air valve knob you should immediately push in the air valve knob, set the gasoline hand gas lever to completely open and at the same time completely depress the starting pedal.**

3

When the motor is running, open the wood-gas lever a little. Let the motor run for at least a minute to suction off any remnant gases that might be present from the gas generator - Otherwise there is danger of explosion in the gas generator

4

Only then hold a burning fuse to the air-ignition hole of the gas generator. Use only wood-wool or newspaper, never gasoline - Danger of explosive ignition.

The motor should now run for 3-4 minutes with gasoline, in neutral, at a high rpm.

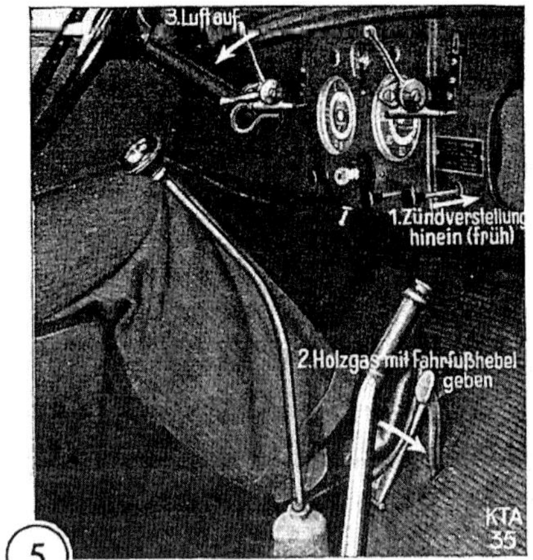

5

1. Ignition timing (early)
2. Increase the introduction of wood gas with the drive pedal
3. Air open

Now, the switch from gasoline operation to wood gas operation takes place, where the individual levers are to be used in the following order:

1. Push in the ignition timing knob all the way. This corresponds to the setting of early ignition.
2. Increase the introduction of wood gas with the driver pedal.
3. **AT THE SAME TIME** open the wood gas/air mixture level far enough that the motor is supplied with a favorable mixture.

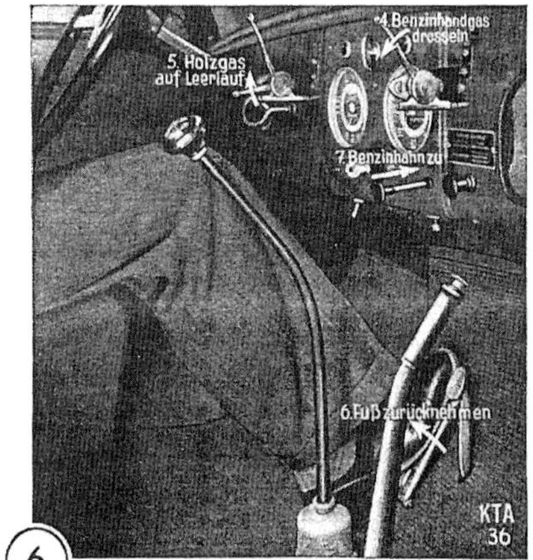

6

4. Turn down the hand gasoline lever 5. Wood gas at neutral 6. Lift up foot.

4. Turn down the gasoline hand gas lever. **BE CAREFUL**

...THAT THE MOTOR DOES NOT STALL!

5. Adjust the motor's idle with the wood gas hand lever and....

6. ...At the same time take your foot from the drive pedal.

7. Push in the gasoline button completely. The gasoline is now completely shut off.

Shortly after starting the wood gas worsens. In order to get past this so called "weak point" it is necessary to give more fuel. If need be give full wood gas and at the same time to close the air adjustment lever a little. When this "weak point" has been passed, the motor should keep running for a while at high rpm.

Once wood gas is properly available and adjusted, your trip can begin.

FAHRBETRIEB — OPERATION

a) normale Fahrt — Normal Driving

1

In a wood gas vehicle, just as in a gasoline powered vehicle, the amount of gas is regulated with the drive pedal.

2

Using the air adjustment lever, adjust the most favorable amount of air, depending on the load and the quality of fuel wood. The air adjustment lever is at the proper setting when it is at the highest setting where the motor pulls well. From time to time during a trip the air setting should be checked and if need be adjusted.

Editors Note: This might also mean exiting the vehicle and adjusting the carbeurator setting.

Refilling the gas producer

GASERZEUGER NACHFÜLLEN,

Restholz im Gaserzeuger

With wood remnants in the generator

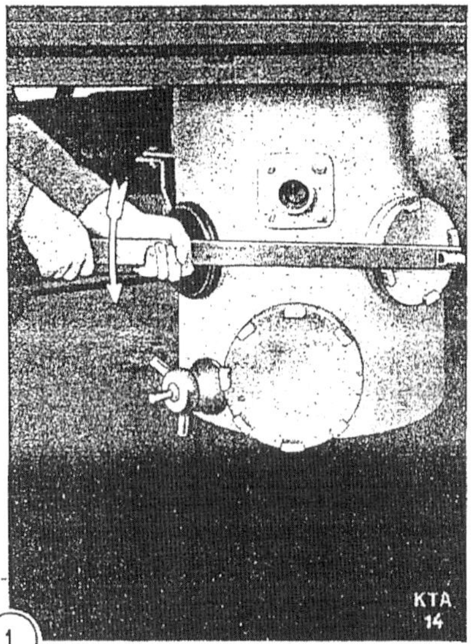

1 Unscrew the upper hatch cover

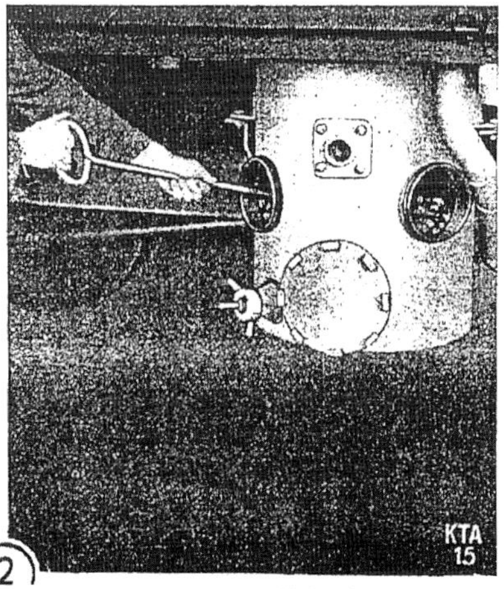

2 Loosen the charcoal with the charcoal rake all around the hearth supports

3 Also loosen up the charcoal under the hearth supports. While doing this, insert the charcoal rake diagonally from above through the upper hatch openings, push the hook of the charcoal rake under the hearthsupports, then move it back and forth.

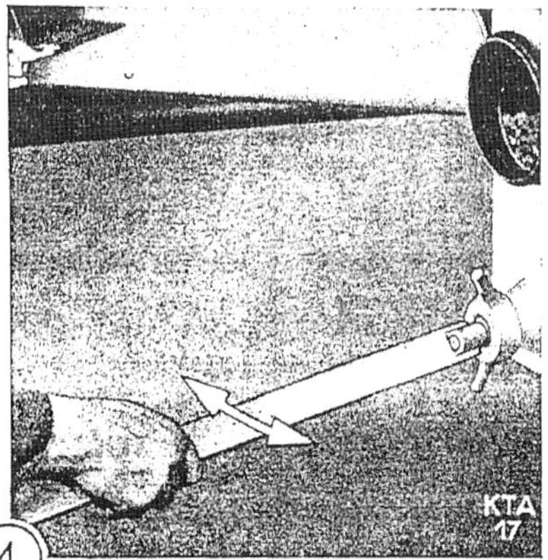

4 Open the threaded cap to the hearth-pin ("ruttledorn") with the hatch-iron, then move the oscillating sleve back and forth three times. Tighten the threaded cap back on

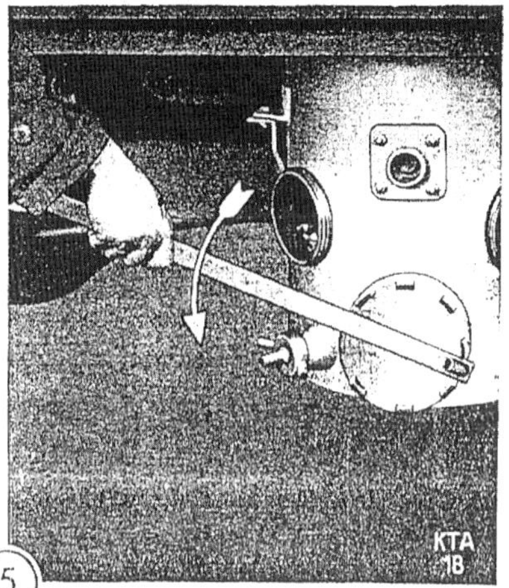

5 Unscrew the lower hatch cover (end cap).

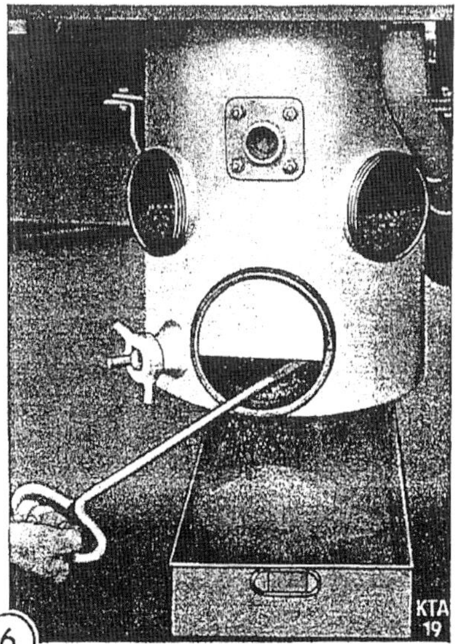

6 Clean out the ashes from the gas-generator using the charcoal rake

7 Add the fuel (in this case charcoal but wood works also) to the correct level up to the middle of the upper hatches.

8 Brush graphite lubricant onto all hatch covers.[1]

1 See earlier note regarding graphite

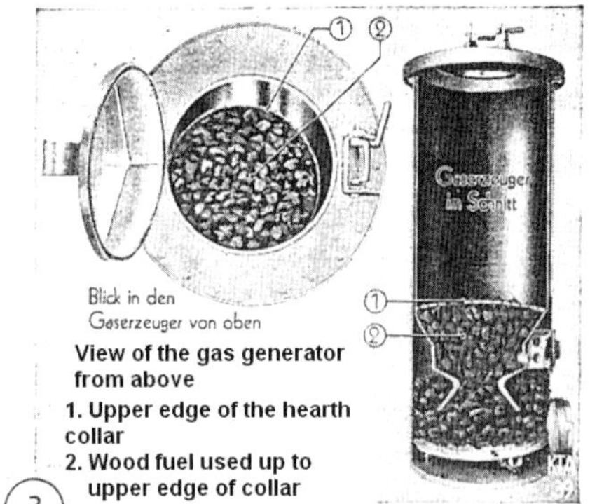

View of the gas generator from above
1. Upper edge of the hearth collar
2. Wood fuel used up to upper edge of collar

(3) Cross section of gas generator

Never let the gas generator run till completely empty, at the most exhaust fuel down to the upper edge of the hearth collar. Add to the wood filling depending on the quality of the wood and the driving conditions every 50 to 70 kilometers. Add wood either with the motor running or if the motor is stopped only with the blower turned on and the shut-off flap open. Doing this will limit the amount of smoke during filling. Never put your face over the filling opening, as flames may jump out of it.

The gas generator should in general be filled all the way up, however, if the motor is to be shut down for a longer break, only put in as much fuel wood as will leave the gas generator at least half full while not in use. This way not too much moisture will accumulate in the gas generator since that would make the fuel too wet for the equipment to start up later.

Hill Driving

When driving uphill it is important to take care that the motor maintains sufficient rpm. In contrast to gasoline engines one should downshift sooner.

Editor's note: There are many anecdotal accounts of drivers having to stop, dismount, and manually stir the firebox, to increase gas production, before attempting a steep hill.

UPHILL: Longer uphill stretches

(1) Shut the air adjustment lever completely. Give some gas with the drive pedal so that the gas generation is not interrupted.

CAUTION: Do not give too much gas, otherwisde (when the air adjustment lever is closed) there will be excessive heating of the gas generator and overly strong buildup of residue.

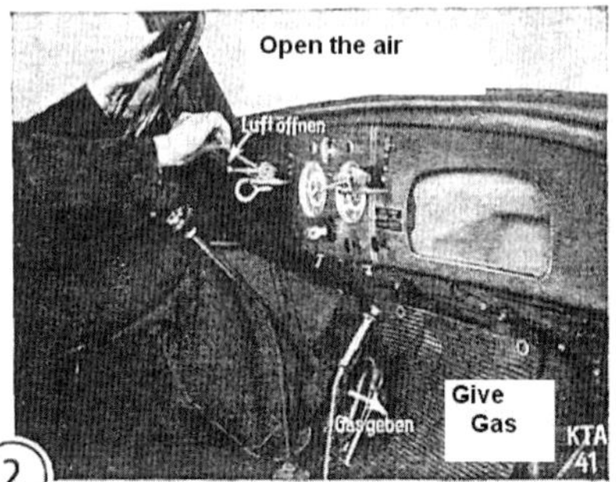

(2) At the end of the downhill stretch open the air adjustment lever just enough so that the motor operates properly. Give gas with the drive pedal.

SPECIAL INSTRUCTIONS FOR PARTICULARLY LONG DOWNHILL STRETCHES

For very long downhill stretches, it is advantageous in order to avoid overheating of the gas generator and excessive build up of residues to interrupt the gas production for most of the downhill passage.

This is done in the following manner: Close completely the air adjustment lever, the wood gas lever, and the foot pedal.

Only a bit before the end of the downhill stretch, give a little with the drive pedal in order to increase gas production to the point needed for the motor to run strongly.

If the driver knows the stretch of road, then he will be able to set the correct adjustments on the basis of experience.

Editor's Note: If the engine is left running, there is danger of CO poisoning if gases build up in the engine compartment and leak into the passenger areas.

(2) 5. After about one minute of it being open, push the knob all the way in. The shut off flap is now fully closed

d) Betriebspausen

Pauses in operation

The motor can be left running in neutral for about 10 minutes. To avoid buildup in the suction pipe, and the formation of a "burn cavity", the motor should be turned off during longer pauses.

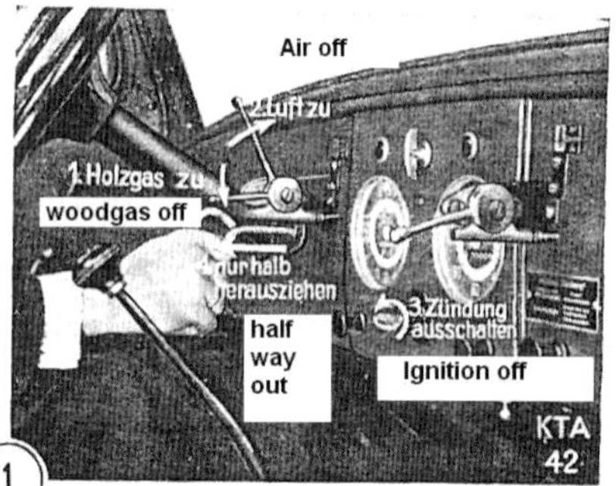

(1) To shut down the engine during longer pauses:
1. Close the wood gas hand lever
2. Close the wood gas air adjustment lever
3. Turn the ignition key to the left ("off")
4. Pull the knob for the shut off flap out to the middle position-Doing this allows wood gas to escape through the exhaust pipe.

(3) If there is a hard freeze, drain the condensed water from the settling tank

A "burn cavity" is an empty space within the wood fill of the gas generator which arises when the vehicle is standing still and the wood fill jams and doesn't slide down. This can also be caused by using the blower too long or leaving the motor running in neutral too long. Dueing travel the wood is continually shaken loose and a "burn cavity" would come about only through using too long and/or bulky pieces of wood. To remove a "burn cavity" the wood fill of the gas generator is lightly poked at with a wooden pole, while taking caution no to damage the inside of the generator.

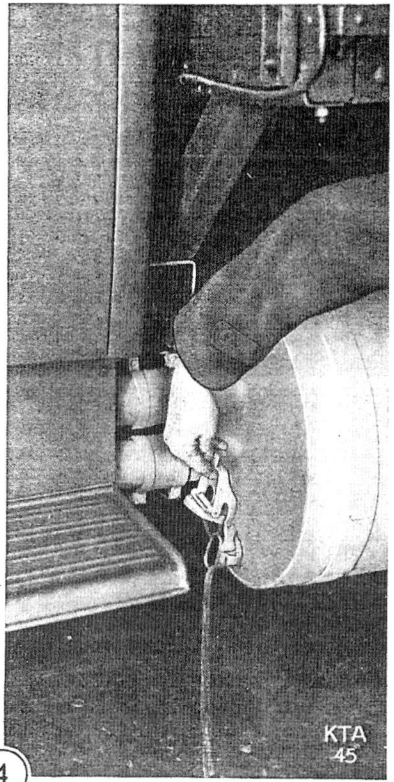

4
empty the condensed water from the filter.

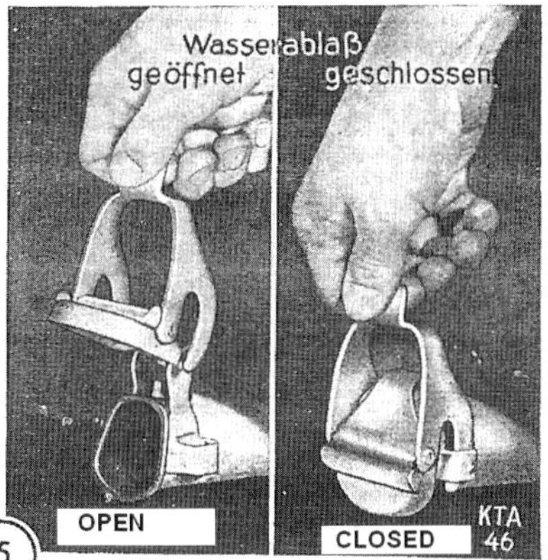

5

e) Wiederanfahren

STARTING UP AGAIN

Nach kurzen Betriebspausen bis etwa 10 Minuten.

After a short pause of up to 10 minutes

Start the motor immediately as per the starting procedure for wood gas.

After longer pauses of up to some 3 hours.

The wood fill in the gas generator should be carefully poked with a wooden pole. This stirring should rekindle the embers. There should be no need for relighting the generator, as it is sufficient to fan the embers still present in the generator by activating the blower.

Then after the wood gas builds up, start the engine.

AFTER LONGER PAUSES IN OPERATION AFTER THE FIRE IN THE GENERATOR HAS DIED OUT.

First of all one should poke the wood fill in the gas generator carefully with a wooden pole, then light the gas generator as per that procedure.

Finally, the motor is to be turned on as per that procedure.

SHUTTING DOWN PROCEDURE AT THE END OF A TRIP

There are no tasks associated with the gas generator and you do not need to refill the fuel wood at this time.

1
Remove both caps from the gas cooler.

2
Open the water valve on the settling container and...

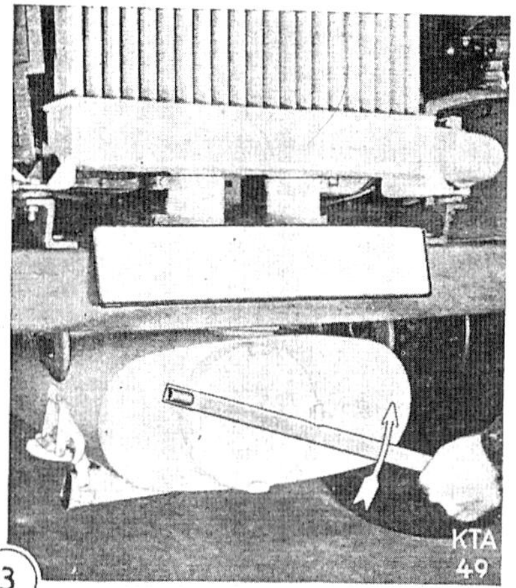

3
...Unscrew the hatch cover from the settling container

4
Rinse out the radiator and the settling container

(5) **Directly rinse the settling container. The rinsing must be done immediately after the trip. if running water is not available, a few buckets of clean water will do.**

(6) **Open the water valve on the filter and drain out the condensed water. The filter does not need to be rinsed out with water. After the water is drained out, the sealing surfaces must be brushed with graphite and resealed.**

WÖCHENTLICHE WARTUNG

WEEKLY MAINTENANCE

CLEAN OUT THE GAS GENERATOR AND REFILL. The entire contents of the COOLED DOWN gas generator must be emptied. It is advisable to run the gas generator before this until it is empty.

Editor's note: This had to be done regardless of mileage, as the products sitting in the firebox, combined with humidity, deteriorated components

(1) For cleaning, open the hinged lid...

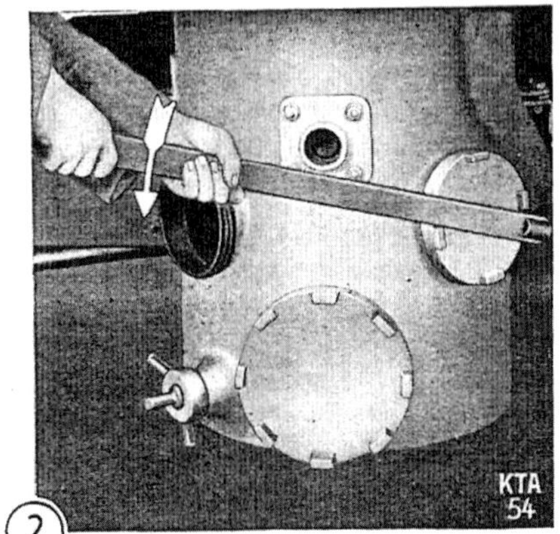

(2) **Unscrew all hatch covers from the gas generator and...**

(3) **...Loosen the threaded cap for the grate pin with the hatch iron 1/2 turn.**

(5) **Clean out the gas generator completely through the lower hatch.**

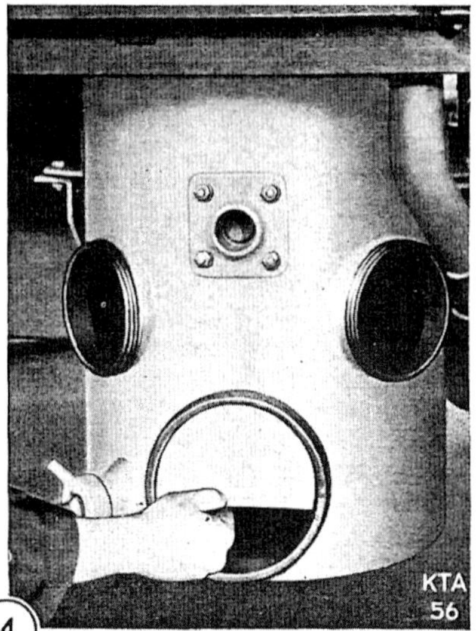

(4) **Take the protective metal sheet out of the lower hatch.**

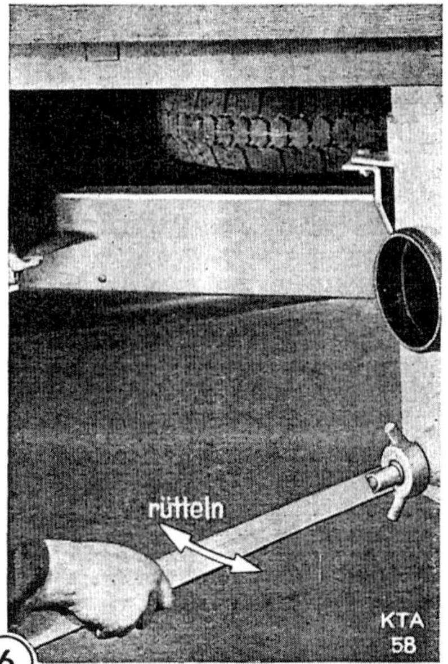

(6) **After the emptying, activate the oscillating sleeve and...**

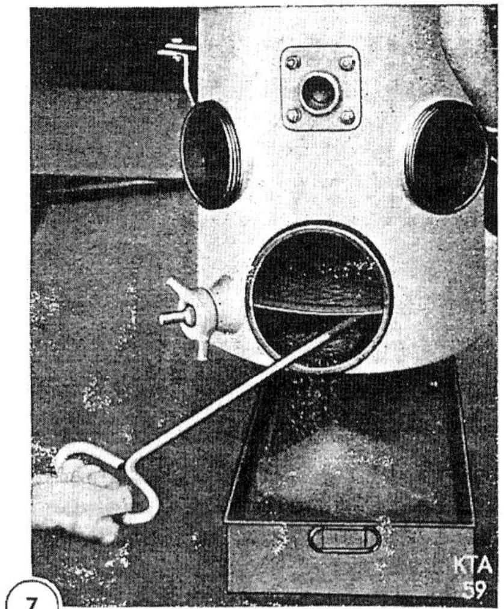

7

...Remove any remaining ashes under the oscillating sieve through the lower hatch

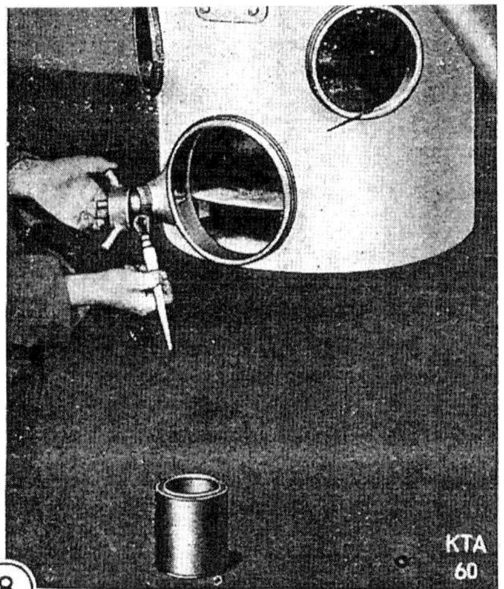

8

Brush the threads of the screw cap and the bearings of the oscillating sieve with graphite lubricant. (see earlier note for production of lubricant)

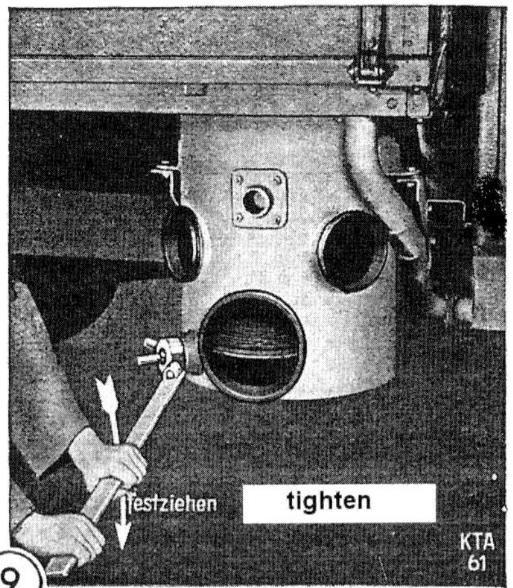

9

Tighten the threaded cap for the grate pin.

Finally, fill up the gas generator immediately for operation.

Open all caps to flush out remaining components of device.

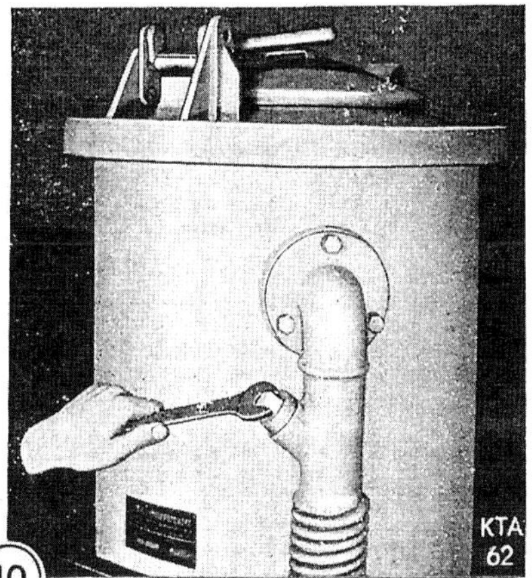

10

Unscrew the rinsing plugs from the pipeline leading out of the top of the gas generator.

11

Unscrew both caps from the gas cooler.

12

Open the water cap on the settling tank and...

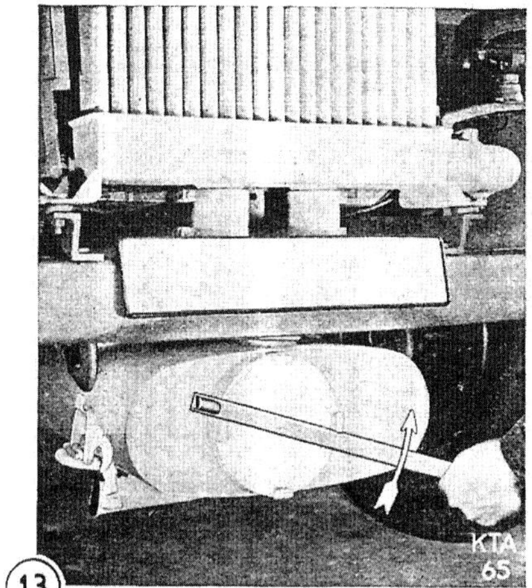

13

Unscrew the hatch cover from the settling tank.

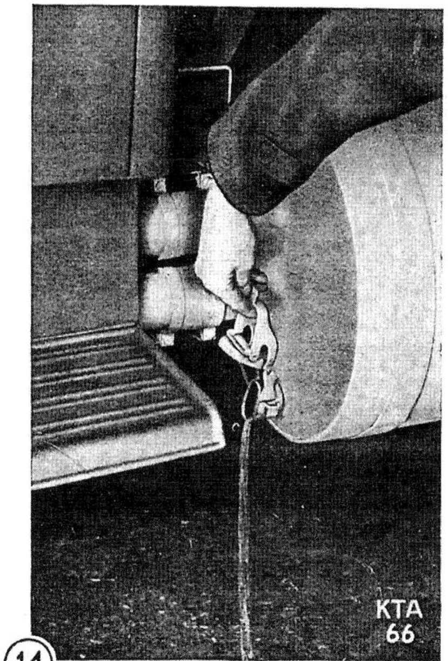

14

Open the water drain on the filter and...

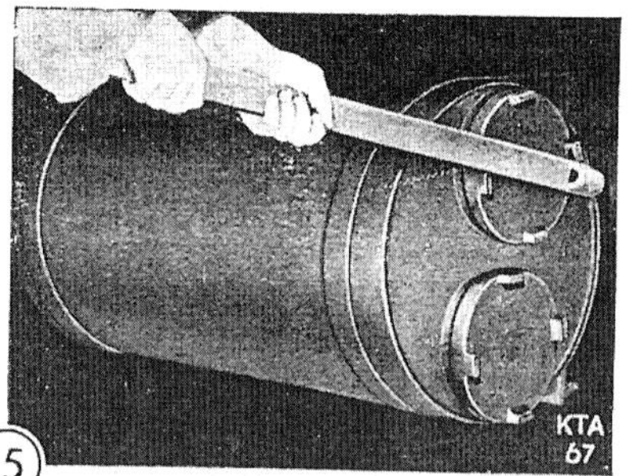

15

Unscrew the upper hatch lid from the filter

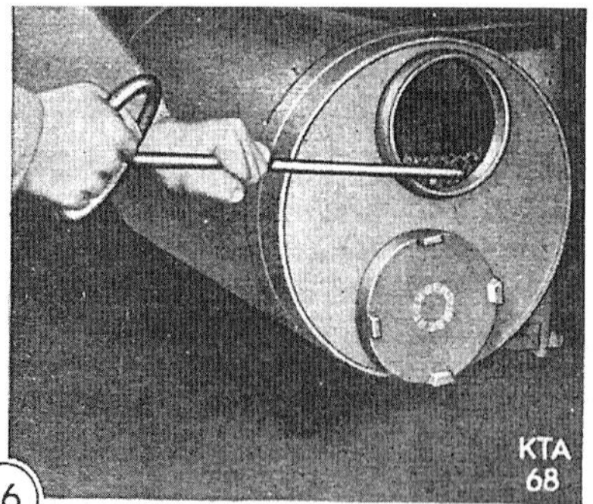

16

Loosen the cork filling of the filter.

17

Unscrew the lower hatch lid on the filter.

FLUSHING OF THE COMPONENTS

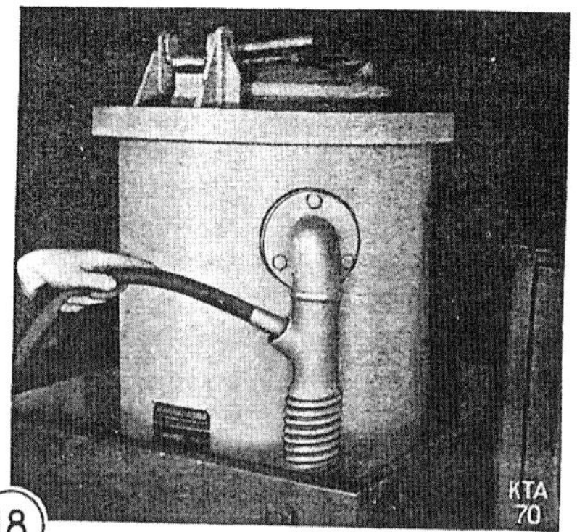

18

Rinse out the pipeline coming out of the top of the gas generator. THE RINSE SHOULD TAKE PLACE DIRECTLY AFTER ENDING A TRIP. If there is no running water available, use several buckets of water.

19

Rinse out the gas cooler. Direct water into all the chambers including those on the sides

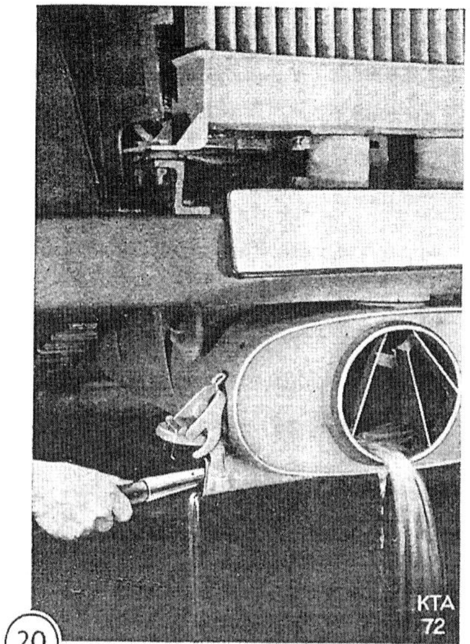

20

Direct water through the drain into the settling tank.

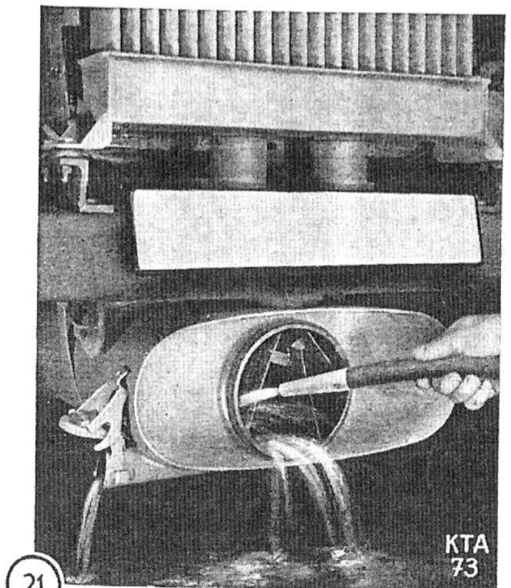

21

Direct water through the hatch opening in the settling tank.

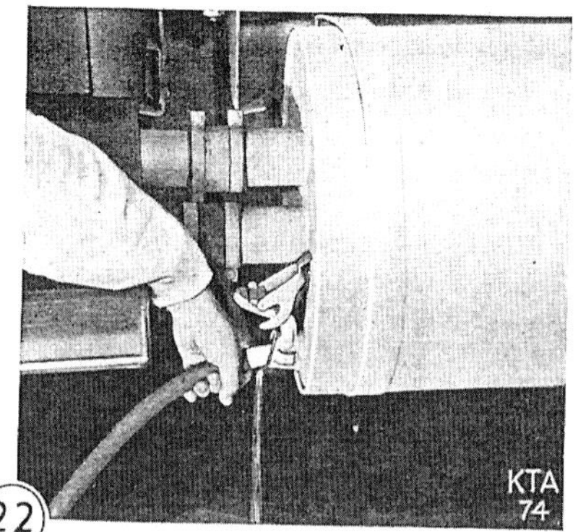

22

Direct water through the drain into the filter.

23

Direct water into the filter through the upper hatch.

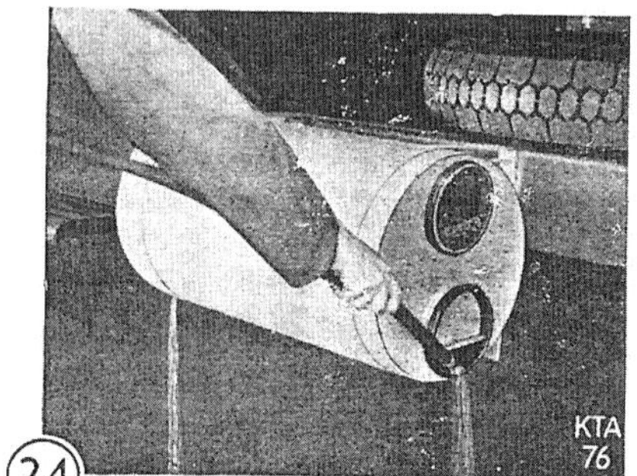

24

Direct water through the lower hatch into the filter.

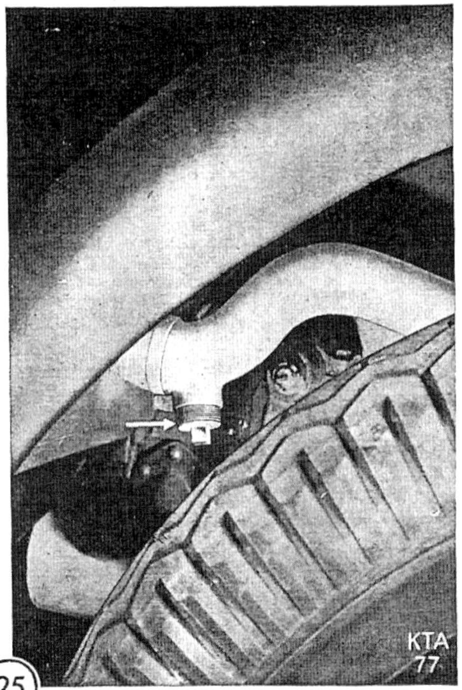

25

Unscrew the water drain plugs from the pipeline beneath the front fender.

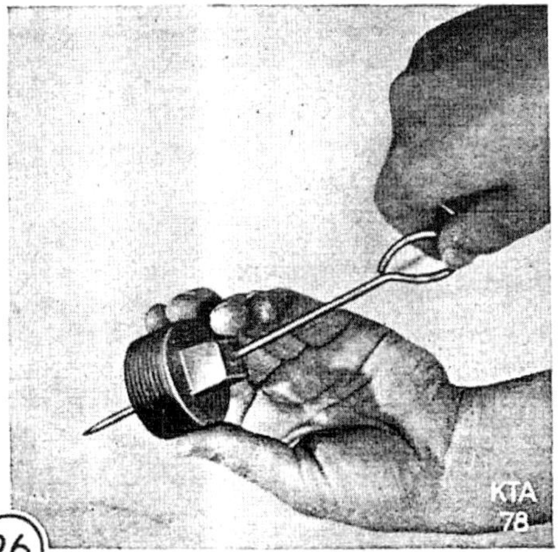

26

Clean out and unplug the drill-hole in the drain plugs.

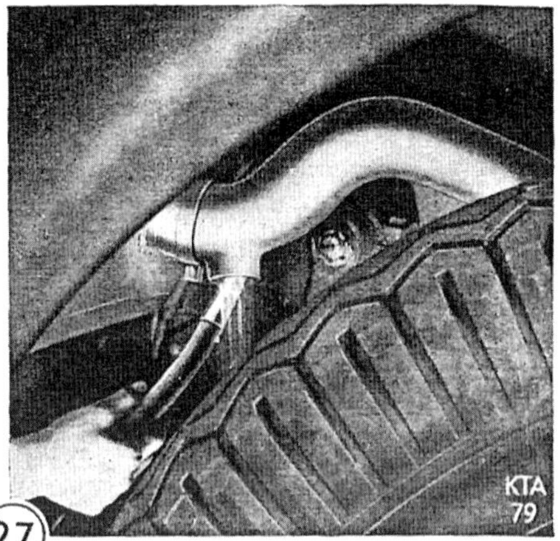

27

Rinse out the pipeline under the left front fender.

After the rinsing water has drained off, all thread surfaces on hatch covers and rinsing plugs as well as the seals of the gasradiator lids are to be brushed with graphite lubricant.

The charge of the battery should be tested at least once a week, and in the event of heavy use, more often. Add only distilled water, never acid, up to some 10 to 15 mm. above the plate edge. If necessary, charge the battery from a different

28

The ongoing maintenance involves changing the cork filling of the filters, oil changes more often than other vehicles and special precautions for winter driving. Suffice it to say, driving these vehicles involved a great deal of inconvenience and intense preventive maintenance.

Bussing-N.A.G truck, 1940. (Reprinted with permission of Diesel Queen pubs.)

Above: German army troops in front of a woodburning bus during a pause. Right: Servicing a woodburning bus.

PANHARD *vous présente son Gazogène pour adaptation aux Voitures de Tourisme et Camionnettes*

L'appareil se compose : 1° d'un Générateur qui peut être placé soit dans une des ailes, soit à l'arrière du véhicule. 2° d'un Epurateur vertical spécial, se plaçant dans l'autre aile ou à l'arrière. Il peut être remplacé, sur demande, par l'épurateur de série horizontal dans le cas de montage à l'arrière. 3° d'un Mélangeur. 4° d'un Dépoussiéreur.

USINE DE TARBES, 19, boulevard Nord de l'Arsenal. Tél. : 1034
Siège social : 19, avenue d'Ivry, PARIS. Tél. : Gob. 65-60

SUCCURSALES :

TOULOUSE, 9, 11 et 13, boulevard Carnot — MARSEILLE, 256, avenue du Prado.
NICE, 35, avenue Georges-Clemenceau. — ALGER, 2, boulevard Camille-Saint-Saëns.
ORAN, 70 avenue Saint-Eugène.

Panhard advertisement.

Really nice French advertisement for wood and coal burning trucks.

References

Automobiletechnisches Handbuch, Bussien et al, Technische Verlag Herbert Cram, Berlin, 1942.

Behandlung und Instandsetzung von Fahrzeug Gaserzeugeranlagen, Heinz Fibelkorn, Verlag Wilhelm Knapp, Halle (Saale) Germany, 1944.

Berliner Morgenpost, October 9, 1942.

Bibliotheque du Chauffer, Les Vehicules Equipes avec Gazogene, Henri Petit, Dunod, Paris, 1941.

Collaboration and Resistance. Pechanski, Durand et al. Harry N. Abrams, New York, New York. 2000.

Economic Survey of Germany, Section D, Fuel, Power and Public Utility Services, British Foreign Office and Ministry of Economic Warfare, Economic Advisory Branch, His Majesty's Printing Office, London, 1944.

Economic Survey of Germany, Section S, Standard of Living and Rationing, British Foreign Office and Ministry of Economic Warfare, *Economic Advisory Branch*, His Majesty's Printing Office, London, 1944.

Fueling the Third Reich, Arnold Krammer, Journal of the Society for the History of Technology, pp 394-422,1978.

Generator Jahrbuch 1942, Ostwald et al, Joh. Kasper & Co, Berlin, 1942.

Horses of the German Army in WWII, Paul L. Johnson, Schiffer Military History, Atglen, PA, 2006.

Lastwagen mit Gasbetrieb, Maschinenfabrik Augsburg Nuremberg, (M.A.N.) Nuremberg, Germany, 1935.

Manuel Pratique des Automobiles a Gazogene, 5th Edition, Etienne Chiron, Editor, 40 Rue de Seine, Paris, 1940.

Oberkommando der Wehrmacht, General der Motorisierung, 12/22/1942.

Sweden, a wartime survey, Government Publication, Swedish Government Printing Office, Stockholm, 1943.

Wood Gas, Wikipedia, the free encyclopedia, online, 10/20/07 1845.